PARTY FOOD

VEGAN

106 party recipes for you, your vegan guests, and anyone who loves great food

Elisa Grelecki

ISBN 979-8-9937209-0-6 hardcover

This book is dedicated to my Guinness girl, who spent countless hours at my feet in the kitchen, making me step over her a million times and hoping for something to drop.

"LIFE WAS MEANT FOR GOOD FRIENDS AND GREAT FOOD." – ANONYMOUS

What does it mean to be vegan? At its simplest, it's a choice to leave animal products off the plate. But the 'why' can differ from person to person. For some, it's an act of compassion for animals; for others, it's a commitment to personal health or a gentler footprint on the Earth.

But 'vegan' isn't a box you have to fit into perfectly. Maybe you're a 'Monday-through-Friday' plant eater or someone who is 'vegan-ish' until a special family celebration comes around. Whether you're all in or just starting to lean in, one universal truth unites us all: our love for delicious food.

Family holiday parties and get-togethers frame some of my favorite memories in life. Everyone squeezed into the kitchen, appetizers scattered across the counter, the rhythmic clinking of glasses, and a football game or a favorite playlist humming in the background.

Why do we always cram into the kitchen? We stand elbow-to-elbow by the stove, even when the living room is empty and there's plenty of room to spread out. Maybe it's to be closer to the food, maybe to each other, or probably both.

Whether you are strictly vegan, 'vegan-curious,' or inviting some of your plant-based friends and relatives to your next party, this book is for you. These recipes aren't just about ingredients; they're about making sure no one is left out of the celebration.

Welcome to the party. There's always room for one more!

Have fun!

WHAT'S ON THE MENU

ORIGINAL
CHOLULA
HOT SAUCE

BRUNCH

TOFU SCRAMBLE

SERVES 4 TO 6

Savory and creamy, this tofu scramble is a must for your next brunch. Pairs perfectly with potato hash, avocado toast, bagels, and mimosas!

¼ cup non-dairy milk
¼ cup vegan mayonnaise
2 tablespoons nutritional yeast
1 tablespoon Dijon mustard
1 teaspoon garlic powder
1 teaspoon turmeric
½ teaspoon onion powder
½ teaspoon pepper
½ teaspoon salt
¼ teaspoon black salt (kala namak)*
1 tablespoon vegan butter
14- to 16-ounce package firm tofu, drained and pressed
14- to 16-ounce package silken tofu, drained and lightly patted dry

Garnish (optional)
Fresh chives, finely chopped
Cherry tomatoes, halved
Avocado, sliced

1. In a small mixing bowl, whisk together the milk, mayonnaise, nutritional yeast, Dijon mustard, garlic powder, turmeric, onion powder, pepper, salt, and black salt. Set aside.
2. Add butter to a large pan and melt over medium heat. Break the firm tofu apart with your hands and add to the pan. Use a spatula to stir the tofu while continuing to break it into smaller pieces until it resembles scrambled eggs.
3. Add the silken tofu to the pan. Break the silken tofu apart with the spatula and incorporate it into the firm tofu.
4. Pour in the seasoning mixture and stir until the tofu is evenly coated.
5. Reduce the temperature to medium-low and cook for an additional 4 to 7 minutes, stirring occasionally, until the liquid has evaporated. Garnish with fresh chopped chives, tomatoes, or avocado.

Note

*Black salt, also called kala namak, has a very sulfurous smell and taste. A little goes a long way. If you've never used it before, it may make you question why we are putting this into food, but trust me, it will make it taste like eggs. Think of it as concentrated egg seasoning. I would start with ¼ teaspoon, and you can add more if you want a stronger egg flavor.

BREAKFAST HASH

SERVES 6 TO 8

I love potatoes. Fry them, mash them, stuff them into dumplings, bake them, I love them all! They're so comforting. These potatoes are full of flavor and just what your brunch needs!

2 pounds russet potatoes, peeled and chopped into approximately ½-inch cubes
2 teaspoons salt, divided
3 tablespoons extra-virgin olive oil, divided
½ green bell pepper, chopped
½ red bell pepper, chopped
½ yellow onion, diced
½ teaspoon black pepper
½ teaspoon garlic powder
½ teaspoon onion powder
½ teaspoon smoked paprika

1. Add potatoes to a pot and add enough water to cover the potatoes by 1 inch.
2. Add 1 teaspoon salt and bring to a boil over medium-high heat. Reduce heat to medium–low and maintain a simmer.
3. Simmer potatoes until they are almost fork tender; do not let them get soft, about 8 to 10 minutes. Start checking them with a fork around 7 minutes.
4. Drain potatoes and set aside to cool. *I recommend lining a baking sheet with aluminum foil and spreading the potatoes out so they can cool quickly and evenly.*
5. Add 1 tablespoon olive oil to a large pan and heat over medium-high heat. Add peppers and onions and cook until they start to get tender, about 4 minutes.
6. Combine the black pepper, garlic powder, onion powder, and smoked paprika in a small bowl. Stir it up and set it aside.
7. Add the remaining 2 tablespoons of oil and the potatoes to the pan with the peppers and onions. Sprinkle ⅓ of the seasoning mix over the hash and stir. Cook hash for another 7 to 10 minutes, stirring occasionally and adding more of the seasoning mix each time. Hash is done when the potatoes are fork-tender and are golden-brown. If the hash is not browning, increase the heat to high for 1 to 2 minutes, stirring every 30 seconds.

Party Tip

Slice up the unused bell peppers and serve them with hummus (pg. 67, 68) or ranch (pg. 147).

BRUNCH EGGLESS ROLLS

MAKES 12 TO 16 ROLLS

Savory and cheesy tofu scramble mixed with mushrooms, onions, and peppers, and wrapped in a crispy egg roll. Pair these with your favorite hot sauces and a bloody Mary!

2 tablespoons vegan butter, divided
1 cup cremini mushrooms, diced
½ cup green bell pepper, diced
½ cup red bell pepper, diced
½ cup yellow onion, diced
¾ teaspoon salt, divided
¼ cup vegan mayonnaise
2 tablespoons nutritional yeast
1 tablespoon Dijon mustard
1 teaspoon garlic powder
1 teaspoon turmeric
½ teaspoon onion powder
½ teaspoon pepper
¼ teaspoon black salt (kala namak)*
14 to 16-ounce package firm tofu, drained and pressed
14 to 16-ounce package silken tofu, drained and lightly patted dry
½ cup vegan shredded cheddar cheese
1 package vegan egg roll wrappers

1. Heat 1 tablespoon of butter in a large pan over medium-high heat.
2. Add mushrooms, peppers, onions, and ¼ teaspoon salt and cook, stirring occasionally, until tender and liquid has evaporated, about 5 to 8 minutes. Transfer to a bowl or plate and set aside.
3. In a small mixing bowl, whisk together the mayonnaise, nutritional yeast, Dijon mustard, garlic powder, turmeric, onion powder, pepper, black salt, and the remaining ½ teaspoon of salt. Set the mixture aside.
4. Add 1 tablespoon of butter to the pan and melt over medium heat. Break the firm tofu apart with your hands and add to the pan. Use a spatula to stir the tofu while continuing to break it into smaller pieces until it resembles scrambled eggs.
5. Add the silken tofu to the pan. Break the silken tofu apart with the spatula and incorporate it into the firm tofu.
6. Pour in the mayonnaise mixture and stir until the tofu is evenly coated. Cook for an additional 5 to 8 minutes, until the liquid has evaporated, stirring occasionally.
7. Add the mushrooms, peppers, onions, and shredded cheese to the pan with the tofu and stir to combine. Remove the pan from heat.
8. Set up your assembly station with the egg roll wrappers, the filling, a plate or tray to place the finished egg rolls, and a small bowl or cup with some water to dip your fingers.
9. Place a wrapper on a clean surface, the points facing up and down (like a diamond), and spoon about ¼ cup of filling in the center of the wrapper.
10. Use a pastry brush or your fingers to brush a small amount of water on the top edge of the wrapper.

recipe continues

recipe continued from previous page

11. Pull the bottom corner of the wrapper up over the filling, then fold each of the sides in, and continue to roll up the wrapper, keeping it tight, until sealed.
12. Set aside, seam side down, and continue with additional wrappers until you've used all the filling.
13. In a frying skillet**, wok, or pot, add 2 to 3 inches of oil and heat over medium heat for about 5 minutes, until 350°F is reached.
14. Carefully add egg rolls into the oil. Cook in batches and make sure not to crowd them, about 3 or 4 at a time. Cook until golden brown and crispy, about 3 to 5 minutes, turning them occasionally to ensure even browning.
15. Carefully remove with a slotted spoon and place on a paper towel-lined plate to drain excess grease. Repeat until all rolls are fried. Serve egg rolls whole or sliced in half with a variety of hot sauces or ketchups.

Notes
*Black salt, also called kala namak, has a very sulfurous smell and taste. A little goes a long way. If you've never used it before, start with ¼ teaspoon, and you can add more if you want a stronger egg flavor.
** To bake the egg rolls, preheat the oven to 400°F and line a baking sheet with parchment paper. Brush or spray each roll with oil and place, seam side down, on the baking sheet. Bake for 8 to 10 minutes, flip, and bake another 8 to 10 minutes, until golden and crispy. Enjoy!

Party tip
Assemble the egg rolls the day before your party but do not cook them. Store them in the refrigerator, seam side down, covered. Make sure to let the filling cool completely before rolling the egg rolls if you intend to make these ahead to prevent the wrappers getting soggy from the steam.

ULTIMATE BRUNCH CASSEROLE

SERVES 8 TO 10

This recipe uses liquid Just Egg. Yes, I name-dropped, but trust me, this will impress, and it's best with this exact brand. Nonvegans will be going back for seconds and thirds! It's comforting, satisfying, and incredibly flavorful. This dish is perfect for a holiday brunch or early tailgate.

1 tablespoon extra-virgin olive oil
1 green bell pepper, diced
1 red bell pepper, diced
1 yellow onion, diced
1 teaspoon garlic powder
½ teaspoon black pepper
½ teaspoon salt
20- to 30-ounce bag frozen shredded hash browns, thawed according to package
1 ½ cups shredded vegan cheddar cheese, divided
1 heaping cup of your favorite vegan breakfast sausage (or regular vegan sausage), cooked to package directions and chopped
2 16-ounce containers of Just Egg* (vegan egg replacement)

Note
*Just Egg is not affiliated with this cookbook or me, and they have not sponsored or endorsed *PARTY FOOD VEGAN.*

1. Preheat oven to 350°F and spray a 9x13 pan (or similar size) with cooking spray.
2. Add olive oil to a large pan and heat over medium heat. Add peppers, onions, garlic powder, black pepper, and salt, and sauté until tender, for about 8 minutes.
3. CASSEROLE ASSEMBLE! Spread out the potatoes evenly on the bottom of the pan, gently pressing them down to form the base.
4. Next sprinkle 1 cup of the cheese on top of the potatoes evenly, again pressing down just slightly.
5. Peppers, onions, and sausage come next. Spread them out evenly on top of the cheese, using a spatula, spoon, or your hands.
6. Shake up the Just Egg and pour each of the containers over the casserole. Once done, lift the dish and gently tap it on the counter a couple times to make everything even.
7. Top with the remaining ½ cup of cheese and place in the oven uncovered. Bake for 55 to 65 minutes, until firm.

Party tip
This casserole can be assembled (without baking) the night before and kept in the refrigerator, covered. The next day, allow the dish to come to room temperature on the counter for about 30 minutes, then bake, uncovered.

DEVILED POTATOES

MAKES 24

This vegan take on a classic appetizer is perfect for brunch, parties, holidays, or potlucks. The creamy, tangy, nostalgic egg flavor is packed into tender potatoes. They taste so close to their egg counterpart, even nonvegans will be going back for more!

12 small white, yellow, or red potatoes
⅓ cup vegan mayonnaise
1 ½ tablespoons nutritional yeast
1 ½ tablespoons yellow mustard
¼ teaspoon black pepper
¼ teaspoon black salt (kala namak)*
¼ teaspoon salt
¼ teaspoon turmeric
Paprika, for garnish

Garnish (optional)
Fresh chives or dill, chopped

Notes
I recommend boiling a few extra potatoes. The scooping process can be a little tricky at first, and you may break a potato or two.
*Black salt (kala namak) has a strong sulfurous smell and taste. Start with ¼ teaspoon, taste the filling, and add another ¼ teaspoon if you want a stronger flavor.

Party tip
Make the potatoes and the filling the day before and store separately in the refrigerator. All that is left to do is top the potatoes with the filling, garnish, and serve!

1. Add potatoes to a pot and cover with water by 1 to 2 inches. Bring to a boil, then reduce heat to medium, and cook until potatoes can be easily pierced with a fork, approximately 15 to 20 minutes.
2. Drain and rinse the potatoes with cool water. Set potatoes aside to continue cooling.
3. Once potatoes are cool enough to handle, cut the potatoes in half, lengthwise.
4. Optional step: Gently peel the skin off the potatoes. The skin should come off easily, but be careful not to break any of the potatoes. This step is optional, as it is more for the presentation than the taste.
5. Using a small spoon or melon baller, carefully scoop out the flesh of the potato halves, making sure to leave a border on the bottom and the sides. Add the potato flesh you are scooping out into a mixing bowl. Repeat with each potato half.
6. Using a fork or potato masher, mash the potato flesh until smooth.
7. Add the mayo, nutritional yeast, mustard, black pepper, black salt, salt, and turmeric to the mixing bowl. Stir until evenly combined.
8. Using a pastry bag or a spoon, squeeze or scoop the filling evenly into the potato shells.
9. Sprinkle paprika on top of each deviled potato. Garnish with fresh chives or dill (optional).

CARROT LOX

SERVES 4 TO 6

Having a bagel station? You need to add carrot "lox". They look and taste like their seafood counterparts. Arrange bagels and vegan cream cheese on a platter with sliced onions, tomatoes, cucumbers, some fresh herbs, capers, and these carrots, and oh yeah—don't forget the bellinis!

4 carrots, washed and peeled
2 teaspoons salt, divided
2 tablespoons caper brine
2 tablespoons dill pickle brine
2 tablespoons fresh dill, finely chopped
2 tablespoons white wine vinegar
1 tablespoon extra-virgin olive oil
½ tablespoon liquid smoke
1 teaspoon lemon juice
1 teaspoon lemon pepper seasoning

1. Shave the carrots into ribbons using a vegetable peeler or a mandoline slicer.
2. Fill a medium or large pot with water and 1 teaspoon of salt and bring to a boil.
3. Add the carrot strips to the pot and boil for 3 minutes. While carrots are boiling, set up a large bowl with ice and water to blanch the carrots.
4. Remove carrots from the hot water and place them immediately into the ice bath for 1 to 2 minutes. Drain and set aside.
5. In a medium bowl, whisk together 1 teaspoon salt, caper brine, pickle brine, dill, white wine vinegar, olive oil, liquid smoke, lemon juice, and lemon pepper seasoning.
6. Add the carrots to the bowl and make sure they are all fully coated.
7. Cover and refrigerate for at least 2 hours, preferably overnight. Once ready to serve, remove carrots from marinade and pat dry.

Party tip

These lox are even better the next day, so make-ahead approved! You can make them up to 5 days in advance.

CHIVE BAGEL SPREAD

SERVES 8 TO 10

Creamy and smooth tofu cream cheese with bursts of fresh chive flavor.

14- to 16-ounce block extra-firm tofu, drained and pressed
½ cup nutritional yeast
¼ cup fresh chives
¼ cup non-dairy milk
1 tablespoon extra-virgin olive oil
1 tablespoon lemon juice
1 teaspoon garlic powder
1 teaspoon onion powder
1 teaspoon salt

1. Add all ingredients to a food processor. Process on low until a smooth texture has been reached, like cream cheese. Make sure to scrape down the sides of the bowl as you blend.
2. Chill in the refrigerator, covered, until ready to serve.

Party tip

Make this up to 4 days before your party and store it, covered, in the refrigerator.

SWEET PEA AVOCADO TOAST

MAKES 12 SLICES

Creamy avocado mixed with sweet peas and fresh dill and topped with everyone's favorite brunch seasoning.

6 slices vegan pumpernickel bread, cut in half (can sub your favorite bread)
2 to 3 tablespoons extra-virgin olive oil
3 avocados, peeled and pitted
1 cup frozen sweet peas, cooked according to package, divided
3 tablespoons fresh dill, finely chopped, divided
1 tablespoon lemon juice
Everything bagel seasoning (about 1 tablespoon)

1. Preheat oven to 400°F and line baking sheet(s) with tin foil.
2. Brush both sides of the bread slices with olive oil and place on a baking sheet. Bake for about 9 to 12 minutes, until the bread is crisp and lightly golden on top.
3. Add the avocado and ¾ cup of the peas to a bowl and mash together using a potato masher or a fork until you get the consistency you like.
4. Stir in 2 tablespoons of the dill and the lemon juice.
5. Spread the avocado and pea mash evenly on toast slices. Top each slice with the remaining ¼ cup peas, 1 tablespoon dill, and a sprinkle of everything bagel seasoning.

Note

If you are not topping with everything bagel seasoning, add ¼ to ½ teaspoon of sea salt to the mash.

STRAWBERRY BALSAMIC AVOCADO TOAST

MAKES 12 SLICES

Creamy avocado topped with fresh strawberries and a balsamic glaze. This is the perfect summer brunch food.

6 slices sourdough bread, cut in half (or sub your favorite bread)
2 to 3 tablespoons extra-virgin olive oil
3 avocados, peeled and pitted
1 tablespoon lemon juice
½ teaspoon sea salt
12 ounces fresh strawberries, sliced
4 to 6 tablespoons balsamic glaze

Garnish (optional)
⅓ cup vegan feta crumbles (pg. 40)

1. Preheat oven to 400°F and line baking sheet(s) with tin foil.
2. Brush both sides of the bread slices with olive oil and place on a baking sheet. Bake for about 9 to 12 minutes, until the bread is crisp and lightly golden on top.
3. Mash the avocado in a bowl using a potato masher or a fork until you get the consistency you like.
4. Stir in the lemon juice and salt.
5. Spread the avocado mash evenly on toast slices. Top each slice with the strawberry slices, a drizzle of balsamic glaze, and vegan feta crumbles (optional).

RASPBERRY STREUSEL

MAKES 12 LARGE BARS OR 24 SMALL BARS

This dish tastes amazing and looks beautiful on your table. Sweet preserves, fresh raspberries, a melt-in-your-mouth buttery crust, and a decadent brown sugar streusel topped with a touch of creamy vanilla icing. Make this vibrant dish for your next brunch or as a dessert for any gathering.

Crust

1 cup vegan butter, melted
½ cup granulated sugar
2 teaspoons pure vanilla extract
½ teaspoon salt
2 cups all-purpose flour

Filling

1 ½ cups raspberry preserves
30 to 36 fresh raspberries

Streusel topping

1 ¼ cup all-purpose flour
½ cup light brown sugar, tightly packed
⅓ cup sugar
½ teaspoon salt
1 teaspoon ground cinnamon
6 tablespoons vegan butter
1 teaspoon vanilla extract

Icing

½ cup powdered sugar
2 ½ teaspoons vanilla-flavored vegan milk or creamer
1 teaspoon vanilla extract

1. Preheat the oven to 300°F and line a 9x13 baking pan (or similar size) with parchment paper. Make sure the parchment paper hangs over the sides so you can easily remove the streusel later. Set aside.
2. Start with the crust. Add the melted butter, sugar, vanilla extract, and salt to a medium bowl and stir together. Add the flour and mix again until everything is evenly combined.
3. Transfer the mixture to the baking pan and spread it out evenly using a spatula or the back of a spoon, gently pressing it down. Bake for 15 minutes.
4. Change the setting on the oven to 350°F.
5. Spread the raspberry preserves on top of the crust and evenly arrange the fresh raspberries on top of the preserves.
6. Next up is the streusel topping. Add the flour, brown sugar, sugar, salt, and cinnamon in a medium bowl and whisk together.
7. In a separate small bowl, melt the butter and stir in the vanilla extract. Drizzle the butter-vanilla mixture over the flour and sugar bowl, lightly mixing just until the flour is absorbed and you get a sand-like, clumpy mixture. Be careful not to overmix.
8. Sprinkle the streusel topping evenly on top of the raspberries. If you mix it a little too much and it resembles more of a paste, don't worry; you can still use this topping, and it will still taste amazing. You will just have to break up pieces and place them evenly over the dish.

recipe continues

recipe continued from previous page

9. Bake for 35 to 40 minutes; you want the filling to bubble on the edges. Remove from the oven and allow it to cool for 25 minutes before lifting the streusel out of the pan, using the parchment paper on the sides.
10. To make the icing, you mix the powdered sugar, plant-based vanilla milk or creamer, and vanilla extract together. Streusel can be enjoyed warm, cooled, or cold. Cut into the size bars you prefer. When you are ready to serve, drizzle the icing on top.

Note

If you want, you can directly switch out the raspberry preserves and fresh raspberries for a different berry: blueberry, blackberry, or strawberry.

Party tip

This streusel can be made up to 4 days before your party and stored in an airtight container in the refrigerator. If you want to serve it warm, reheat it in the oven at 350°F for 10 to 15 minutes.

CINNAMON SWIRL BREAKFAST CAKE

SERVES 8 TO 10

This cake goes amazing with coffee and mimosas. The combination of sweet cinnamon and brown sugar is so comforting and delicious. Bonus: it will make your home smell amazing!

Cake

1 tablespoon vegan butter
2 tablespoons flaxseed meal
6 tablespoons water
2 cups all-purpose flour
1 cup brown sugar
1 tablespoon baking powder
A pinch of salt
1 cup non-dairy milk
1 ½ teaspoon vanilla extract

Cinnamon swirl

½ cup brown sugar
2 tablespoons ground cinnamon
¼ cup vegan butter, melted

Party Tip

This cake can be made ahead of time and stored at room temperature, tightly wrapped, for up to 3 days. You can also store it in the refrigerator, in an airtight container, for up to 5 days (first allow the cake to cool completely). If you would like to reheat the cake, warm it in the oven at 300°F for 5 to 8 minutes. Make sure to cover the pan with aluminum foil before heating so it doesn't dry out.

1. Preheat oven to 350°F and grease a 9x13-inch (or similar size) baking dish with butter.
2. In a small bowl, add the flaxseed and water. Stir together and let sit for at least 5 minutes. This will be your flax egg.
3. In a large mixing bowl, add the flour, brown sugar (1 cup), baking powder, and salt. Stir until evenly combined.
4. In a separate bowl, whisk together the milk, flax egg mix, and vanilla.
5. Add the wet ingredients into the large mixing bowl with the dry ingredients. Stir until completely combined and the mixture is smooth and resembles cake batter.
6. Spread the cake mixture out evenly into the baking dish. Smooth the top with the back of a spoon or a spatula.
7. To make the cinnamon swirl topping, stir together the brown sugar (½ cup) and cinnamon in a mixing bowl. Pour in the melted butter and stir again. It should look like wet sand.
8. Spoon the cinnamon sugar evenly over the cake batter. Using a pointed edge (like a toothpick or the tip of a knife), make circles or swirls with the cinnamon sugar on the top of the cake.
9. Bake for 30 to 35 minutes. Check with a toothpick in the center of the cake; it should come out clean. Let stand for about 10 minutes before serving.

BLOODY MARY STATION

MAKES 6 COCKTAILS

This Bloody Mary station will be the centerpiece of your brunch!

Bloody Mary
32 ounces tomato juice
2 tablespoons lemon juice
2 tablespoons lime juice
2 tablespoons olive brine
2 tablespoons vegan Worcestershire sauce
1 ½ tablespoons horseradish
2 teaspoons Tabasco sauce
1 teaspoon celery salt
1 teaspoon dried basil
1 teaspoon dried oregano
1 teaspoon garlic powder
1 teaspoon Old Bay seasoning
½ teaspoon black pepper
Ice
12 ounces vodka or blanco tequila, divided

1. In a large pitcher, stir together all Bloody Mary ingredients except the ice and vodka or tequila. Cover and chill in the refrigerator for at least 1 hour, or overnight.
2. When you are ready to serve, set up your station with your Bloody Mary mix, vodka or tequila, lemon or lime wedges, rim seasoning, flavor enhancers, and garnishes.
3. Rub each glass rim with a lemon or lime wedge and then dip into one of the rim options.
4. Fill glasses with ice and add 2 ounces of vodka or tequila.
5. Top with Bloody Mary mixture.
6. Have your guests add optional flavor enhancers and garnishes. Cheers!

Rims
1. Mix seasonings together and transfer to a small plate.

Party tip
This cocktail tastes even better when allowed to chill in the refrigerator. Make up to 24 hours before your brunch and keep in the refrigerator, covered.

ingredients continue

recipe continued from previous page

Old Bay rim (optional)
2 tablespoons Old Bay
1 tablespoon coarse sea salt
Lemon or lime wedges

Spicy salt rim (optional)
2 tablespoons coarse sea salt
2 teaspoons celery salt
1 teaspoon garlic powder
1 teaspoon onion powder
1 teaspoon smoked paprika
Lemon or lime wedges

Tajin rim (optional)
2 tablespoons Tajin
1 tablespoon coarse sea salt
Lemon or lime wedges

Flavor enhancers (optional)
Celery salt
Ground pepper
Horseradish
Hot sauces
Old Bay seasoning
Vegan Worcestershire sauce

Garnishes (optional)
Celery stalks
Cherry or grape tomatoes
Cucumbers, sliced
Lemon and lime wedges
Mini vegan grilled cheese sandwiches (pg. 111)
Olives
Pickles, spears, sliced, or mini
Tater tots
Tofu
Vegan bacon
Vegan cheddar cheese, cubed (pg. 41)
Vegan meatballs

MIMOSA GEL SHOTS

MAKES ABOUT 14 TO 18 SHOTS

Bite-size, wiggly, jiggly, refreshing, nostalgic, melt-in-your-mouth treats that taste just like everyone's favorite brunch cocktail.

1 cup orange juice
2 tablespoons sugar
1 ½ teaspoons agar agar powder
1 cup champagne
2 tablespoons triple sec

1. Add orange juice, sugar, and agar agar powder to a medium saucepan and stir to combine.
2. Bring to a boil on medium heat, stirring frequently.
3. Reduce to low and simmer for 5 minutes.
4. Turn off heat and stir in vodka and triple sec.
5. Pour into gelatin shot cups or molds and allow them to set in the refrigerator for 4 hours or overnight.

Party tip

Make these fun boozy treats up to 3 days before your party and keep them in the refrigerator covered.

CHARCUTERIE BOARD

MUSHROOM PÂTÉ

SERVES 6 TO 8

Savory blend of mushrooms, fresh herbs, and garlic. The walnuts help provide that classic texture; you are not going to miss the meat version.

2 tablespoons extra-virgin olive oil
1 yellow onion, roughly chopped
3 garlic cloves
8 ounces baby portabella mushrooms, sliced
(can sub cremini or white mushrooms)
½ cup fresh parsley
3 tablespoons fresh rosemary
1 tablespoon soy sauce
1 teaspoon black pepper
1 teaspoon salt
½ teaspoon poultry seasoning
¼ teaspoon nutmeg
2 bay leaves
1 cup walnuts

1. Add oil to a large pan and heat over medium heat.
2. Add onions and garlic and sauté, stirring occasionally, until onions become translucent, approximately 5 to 7 minutes.
3. Add the mushrooms, parsley, rosemary, soy sauce, pepper, salt, poultry seasoning, nutmeg, and bay leaves (keep the bay leaves whole because you will be removing them). Cook, stirring occasionally, until the mushrooms cook down, about another 4 to 6 minutes.
4. Remove from heat and discard the bay leaves. Transfer the mushroom mixture to a food processor and add the walnuts.
5. Pulse until the mixture becomes the texture you like for your pâté. *Some like a chunky, more coarse texture; I prefer a smooth texture.*
6. Transfer the pate to a small serving container. Gently press it down and smooth the top with a spatula or knife. Chill in the refrigerator for at least 3 hours before serving.

Party tip

Make ahead approved—this dish tastes even better the next day! Store in the refrigerator, covered.

SEITAN SAUSAGE

MAKES 2 SAUSAGE LINKS

Take your vegan charcuterie board to the next level with this vegan sausage. With its meaty texture and savory spices, even your meat-eating friends will be impressed.

1 tablespoon extra-virgin olive oil
1 cup yellow onion, chopped
3 garlic cloves, minced
1 cup canned lentils, drained and rinsed
2 tablespoons soy sauce (can sub tamari or coconut aminos)
1 tablespoon liquid smoke
2 tablespoons nutritional yeast
1 tablespoon poultry seasoning
2 teaspoons smoked paprika
½ teaspoon black pepper
1 cup vital wheat gluten

Note
You can steam the seitan using a bamboo steam basket if you prefer.

Party tip
This sausage can be made up to 5 days in advance of your party and stored in the refrigerator in an airtight container.

1. Heat olive oil in a pan over medium-high heat. Add onions and sauté until translucent, for about 5 to 7 minutes.
2. Add garlic and sauté for another minute, stirring frequently so the garlic does not burn.
3. Reduce heat to medium and add the lentils, soy sauce, and liquid smoke and cook for another 2 minutes.
4. Transfer onion mixture to a food processor. Add the nutritional yeast, poultry seasoning, smoked paprika, and pepper and process until well combined and almost a paste; you still want some texture to the mix.
5. Add the vital wheat gluten and pulse until the vital wheat gluten has been distributed throughout the mixture. Do not overmix; the seitan will be chewy.
6. Lay out a piece of parchment paper or tin foil on the counter and dump the seitan dough onto it. Form the dough into 2 log shapes. Wrap each sausage log in tin foil, leaving a little room for the sausage to expand.
7. Now we are going to steam them! Put a steamer basket in a large pot and add a few inches of water, making sure the water does not touch the bottom of the steamer basket.
8. Bring the water to a boil. Place the seitan pieces in the basket, cover, and steam for 20 minutes.
9. After 20 minutes, carefully flip the seitan pieces over, using tongs. Be careful of the steam! Steam for another 15 minutes. Remove the "sausage" seitan from the aluminum foil and allow it to cool. Add to your charcuterie board or store in the refrigerator until ready to serve.

MARINATED TOFU BITES

SERVES 10 TO 16

These tofu bites are bursting with the same fresh garlic and herb flavor as their mozzarella counterparts. You would never know you were eating tofu. Don't forget the bread, you're going to want every last drop of this marinade!

1 block extra-firm tofu (14 to 16 ounces), drained and pressed
¾ cup extra-virgin olive oil
2 tablespoons fresh basil, finely chopped
2 tablespoons fresh parsley, finely chopped
2 tablespoons sun-dried tomatoes packed in oil, drained and finely chopped
3 garlic cloves, minced
1 teaspoon apple cider vinegar
1 teaspoon fresh oregano, finely chopped
1 teaspoon salt
½ to 1 teaspoon crushed red pepper flakes
½ teaspoon black pepper

1. Cut the tofu into bite-size cubes and transfer them to a sealable container. 1 block of tofu can give you 32 to 64 cubes depending on how big or small you want the bites.
2. Combine the olive oil, basil, parsley, sun-dried tomatoes, garlic, vinegar, oregano, salt, crushed red pepper, and pepper in a mixing bowl and whisk together.
3. Pour marinade over the tofu. Gently stir to fully coat the tofu and chill in the refrigerator, covered, for at least 4 hours, preferably overnight.
4. Let the dish come to room temperature for about 30 minutes before serving. Transfer to a serving dish, including extra marinade *(especially if you are serving with bread—you're going to want to dip it!).*

Party tip
Make-ahead alert! It tastes better the next day!

OLIVE TAPENADE

SERVES 6 TO 8

This bold and savory appetizer has 3 types of olives, sundried tomatoes, fresh herbs, and garlic. Perfect to serve for brunch alongside bloody marys or for a holiday party with martinis, or any time you want an easy, make-ahead, delicious appetizer.

2 garlic cloves, peeled
1 cup pitted green olives
1 cup pitted Kalamata olives
½ cup pitted black olives
¼ cup fresh parsley, roughly chopped
3 tablespoons sun-dried tomatoes packed in olive oil, roughly chopped
2 tablespoons capers
1 tablespoon extra-virgin olive oil
1 tablespoon lemon juice (about ½ lemon)
2 teaspoons dried oregano
½ teaspoon black pepper
Salt to taste

1. Add garlic to a food processor or blender and pulse, in short 2-second intervals, until finely minced. Be careful not to pulse into a paste.
2. Add the remaining ingredients and pulse a few times, again in short 2-second intervals, until evenly combined and pieces are finely chopped. Be careful not to chop too much, or you will have a paste consistency.
3. Taste and add salt to taste: olives, sun-dried tomatoes, and capers contain salt, so this may not be needed.
4. Transfer to your serving bowl and enjoy!

Party tip

Olive tapenade can be made up to 3 days in advance and stored, in an airtight container, in the refrigerator. It does last longer than that, but since we are using fresh herbs, you want your guests to enjoy them at their best. Let the dish come to room temperature for about 30 minutes before serving.

HERB GOAT CHEESE

MAKES 2 CHEESE LOGS

Creamy and tangy tofu cheese infused with fresh herbs.

16 ounces extra-firm tofu, drained and pressed
⅔ cup fresh parsley, finely chopped
½ cup coconut milk
⅓ cup refined coconut oil
¼ cup fresh chives, finely chopped
2 tablespoons fresh thyme, finely chopped
2 tablespoons lemon juice
2 tablespoons white miso paste
1 tablespoon apple cider vinegar
1 tablespoon extra-virgin olive oil
1 tablespoon nutritional yeast
2 teaspoons sea salt
1 teaspoon garlic powder
1 teaspoon ground black pepper

1. Add all your ingredients to a food processor or blender and blend for about 5 minutes, starting with pulses, then a low setting, and eventually high, until it is creamy and smooth. Scrape the sides as needed.
2. Transfer cheese mix to an airtight container and chill in the refrigerator for at least 6 hours, or overnight.
3. After the cheese has chilled and set, you can mold it into logs. This step is optional. You can also serve it from a container as a spread. To make the logs, lay out 2 sheets of plastic wrap. Divide the cheese mixture in half. Shape each half into a log on the plastic wrap using your hands. Wrap the logs in the wrap to maintain the shape.
4. Chill in the refrigerator for another hour for the shape to set or until ready to serve.

Party tip

Make this vegan goat cheese 1 or 2 days before your party and store it, wrapped tightly in plastic wrap, in the refrigerator.

EVERYTHING BAGEL CHEESE BALL

SERVES 10 TO 12

This cheese ball gets its creaminess from coconut milk and cashews, making it rich and decadent. Rolled in everyone's favorite bagel seasoning, this is sure to be a hit at any party.

1 cup raw unsalted cashews
1 cup canned coconut milk*
2 tablespoons white miso paste
1 tablespoon lemon juice
1 tablespoon nutritional yeast
1 teaspoon salt
½ teaspoon black pepper
½ teaspoon garlic powder
½ teaspoon onion powder
1 tablespoon agar agar powder
½ cup everything bagel spice

1. Add the cashews to a bowl and cover with just-boiled water. Let sit for 1 hour, then drain.
2. Add the cashews, coconut milk, miso, lemon juice, nutritional yeast, salt, black pepper, garlic powder, and onion powder to a high-speed blender or food processor. Blend until smooth, scraping down the sides of the blender as you go to incorporate everything. If you tend to adjust recipes and make them more salty or garlicky, etc., now is the time to taste it and adjust if necessary.
3. Add the agar agar powder and blend again to evenly combine.
4. Pour the cheese mixture into a medium saucepan and heat over medium heat. Bring to a low boil while stirring frequently. Boil for 5 minutes while continuing to stir to prevent sticking.
5. Pour cheese sauce into a glass or ceramic container and cool on the counter for 10 minutes, then cover and place in the refrigerator.
6. Refrigerate for about an hour. You do not want it to set all the way.
7. Lay a piece of plastic wrap on the counter and plop the cheese on top in the middle. You may need to use a silicone spatula or a butter knife to scrape the edges of the bowl to get the cheese to pop out.

recipe continues

recipe continued from previous page

8. Grab the corners of the wrap and bunch them together at the top. Gently, using your hands, form the cheese into a ball. It doesn't have to be perfect or the smoothest; we're going to cover it in spices. Twist the plastic wrap to secure the ball, place the ball of wrapped cheese back in the refrigerator, twist-side down so it does not open. Refrigerate at least 8 hours, but preferably overnight.
9. When you are ready to serve, pour everything bagel spice on a plate. Remove the cheese from the wrap carefully, then gently roll it around in the spices until the entire ball is covered.

Note

*Make sure to stir the can of coconut milk before measuring out 1 cup if the fat has separated at the top.

Party tip

Make this cheese up to 4 days in advance of your party and store it, in an airtight container, in the refrigerator. Roll it in the seasoning just before serving.

TOFU FETA

MAKES 2 ½ CUPS

Crumbled tofu marinated in a salty, tangy dressing. Add it to your charcuterie board, bruschetta, avocado toast, crostini, salads, pasta salads, pizza, burgers, or anywhere that you would use feta.

14 to 16 ounces extra-firm tofu (can sub firm), drained, pressed, and patted dry
2 tablespoons white miso
1 tablespoon green olive brine
1 tablespoon nutritional yeast
1 tablespoon squeezed lemon juice
2 teaspoons red wine vinegar
½ teaspoon garlic powder
½ teaspoon salt

1. Crumble the tofu into small pieces with your hands. Set aside.
2. Whisk together the remaining ingredients in a bowl or container.
3. Add the tofu to the marinade and gently stir until all the tofu is coated.
4. Cover and place in the refrigerator for at least 4 hours, preferably overnight.

Party tip

This feta tastes better on day 2 and can be made up to 4 days in advance of your party and stored in the refrigerator.

VEGAN CHEDDAR CHEESE

MAKES 1 BLOCK OF "CHEESE"

Cheddar cheese is a charcuterie board staple. This vegan version is creamy and savory and slices just like its dairy counterpart.

13.5-ounce can coconut milk
½ cup water
⅓ cup nutritional yeast
2 tablespoons agar agar powder
1 tablespoon tahini
2 teaspoons lemon juice
1 ½ teaspoons salt
1 teaspoon garlic powder
1 teaspoon onion powder
1 teaspoon smoked paprika
½ teaspoon turmeric

1. Decide what container you are using for your cheese; it will be the shape of the container. Spray the mold with oil or line the container with parchment paper *(if you are using a glass or ceramic container, I suggest using parchment paper)*.
2. Add all the ingredients to a medium saucepan and stir to combine.
3. Heat on medium and bring to a low boil, stirring frequently. Boil for 5 minutes while continuing to stir to prevent sticking.
4. Pour cheese sauce into the mold and leave out on the counter to cool for 10 minutes.
5. Cover the container and place it in the refrigerator to chill for at least 3 hours, until ready to serve.
6. When ready to serve, pop the cheese out of the mold, or lift it out by pulling up on the parchment paper.

Party tip

Make this cheese up to 4 days in advance of your party and store it, in an airtight container, in the refrigerator.

SALADS AND SIDES

STRAWBERRY CUCUMBER SALAD

SERVES 6 TO 8

Fresh strawberries, cucumbers, and mint. This light and refreshing salad is perfect for summer days or nights.

1 pound strawberries, quartered
1 large cucumber, chopped
½ red onion, finely chopped
⅓ cup vegan feta cheese, crumbled or chopped (store-bought or pg. 40), (can sub 1 large avocado, chopped)
¼ cup fresh mint, finely chopped
2 tablespoons balsamic vinegar
2 tablespoons extra-virgin olive oil
1 tablespoon lemon juice
¼ teaspoon black pepper
¼ teaspoon salt

Garnish (optional)
Balsamic glaze

1. Add the strawberries, cucumber, red onion, feta, and mint to a large mixing bowl and gently stir to combine.
2. In a separate bowl, whisk together the balsamic vinegar, olive oil, lemon juice, pepper, and salt.
3. Pour dressing over salad and gently stir to combine.
4. Transfer to a serving bowl or plate and top with a balsamic glaze drizzle (optional).

MEXICAN CHOPPED SALAD WITH CILANTRO AVOCADO DRESSING

SERVES 6 TO 8

This salad is fresh, delicious, healthy, and vibrant, covered in a creamy dressing with a slight kick. Perfect all year long but especially in the summer served with margaritas!

Dressing
1 cup fresh cilantro
⅓ cup extra-virgin olive oil
⅓ cup water
1 large avocado, pitted and peeled
1 small jalapeño, deseeded
2 tablespoons fresh lime juice
1 garlic clove, peeled
½ teaspoon black pepper
½ teaspoon salt

Salad
1 head romaine lettuce, chopped
15 ounces canned whole kernel corn, drained and rinsed
1 medium orange bell pepper, chopped (can sub any bell pepper color)
1 cup cherry tomatoes, halved
½ medium red onion, chopped
1 jalapeño, diced (omit if you do not like spicy)

Garnish (optional)
½ to 1 cup vegan tortilla strips

1. Using a high-speed blender or food processor, add all dressing ingredients and blend until smooth.
2. In a large mixing bowl, add all salad ingredients (except tortilla strips) and gently mix.
3. Pour dressing over salad and gently toss to evenly coat salad.
4. Transfer salad to serving bowl or plate and top with tortilla chips (optional).

Party tip
Make the dressing the day before and store it in an airtight container in the refrigerator. Place plastic wrap directly on the top of the dressing to minimize air exposure and prevent browning.
You can also prepare the veggies for the salad the day before and store them in separate containers in the refrigerator.

GREEN GODDESS SALAD

SERVES 6 TO 8

Vibrant, creamy, tangy, loaded with herbs, and sure to be a hit!

Dressing

1 cup fresh basil
1 cup fresh cilantro
1 cup fresh dill
1 cup fresh parsley
1 cup vegan plain yogurt
2 tablespoons lemon juice
1 garlic clove
½ tablespoon extra-virgin olive oil
1 teaspoon agave nectar
½ teaspoon black pepper
½ teaspoon salt

Salad

4 cups green leaf lettuce
1 cup frozen shelled edamame, thawed
1 cup microgreens
1 medium green bell pepper, chopped
¾ cup cucumber, chopped
⅓ cup red onion, chopped
¼ cup pistachios shelled (roasted or salted is up to you, *I use salted*)
1 avocado, pitted, peeled, and sliced

1. To make the dressing, add all ingredients to a high-power blender and blend until smooth. Chill in the refrigerator in an airtight container until ready to use.
2. To make the salad, combine all ingredients except the avocado.
3. Pour the green goddess dressing on and gently toss to evenly coat.
4. Transfer to a serving bowl or platter and top with avocado slices.

Party tip

Make the dressing up to 3 days in advance and store it in an airtight container in the refrigerator.

WALDORF SALAD

SERVES 4 TO 6

Tart and crisp apples, sweet grapes, refreshing celery, and crunchy walnuts, all brought together in a creamy dressing. Oldie but a goodie.

1 Granny Smith apple, diced
1 Red Delicious apple, diced
1 tablespoon sugar
2 teaspoons lemon juice
1 cup celery, diced
1 cup red grapes, halved
½ cup walnuts, roughly chopped
½ cup plain vegan yogurt, unsweetened
¼ cup vegan mayonnaise
½ teaspoon salt

1. Add the apples, sugar, and lemon juice to a large mixing bowl and stir until evenly coated.
2. Next add the celery, grapes, and walnuts and gently mix.
3. In a separate small bowl, mix the yogurt, mayonnaise, and salt. Add yogurt dressing to the salad and gently toss until thoroughly combined.
4. Chill in the refrigerator for at least 1 hour before serving.

WHITE BEAN AND HERB SALAD

SERVES 6 TO 8

This satisfying salad combines arugula, cannellini beans, and red onion with fresh parsley, dill, and lemon dressing.

6 tablespoons extra-virgin olive oil
¼ cup fresh parsley, finely chopped
2 tablespoons lemon juice
1 tablespoon fresh dill, finely chopped
1 garlic clove, pressed or minced
½ teaspoon pepper
½ teaspoon salt
2 15-ounce cans cannellini beans, drained and rinsed
½ cup red onion, chopped
4 to 5 cups arugula

1. In a large mixing bowl, whisk together the olive oil, parsley, lemon juice, dill, garlic, pepper, and salt.
2. Add beans and onions and stir until fully coated. Chill in the refrigerator for at least an hour.
3. Place arugula on a serving plate or bowl.
4. Top with beans and dressing.

Party tip

Make this dish, without the arugula, the night before your party. Store in the refrigerator in an airtight container. Simply plate it on the arugula when it is time to serve.

PEAR AND WALNUT SALAD WITH GINGER SESAME VINAIGRETTE

SERVES 6 TO 8

Fresh greens are decorated with sweet cranberries and pears and crunchy walnuts and red onions. Topped with a zesty dressing. This salad looks and tastes amazing.

4 to 5 cups mixed spring greens
1 cup microgreens
½ cup dried cranberries (can sub dried cherries or pomegranate arils)
⅓ cup walnuts (optional step to toast below)
¼ cup red onion, diced
¼ cup vegan feta crumbles (store-bought or pg. 40)
2 pears, sliced

Dressing

⅓ cup extra-virgin olive oil
2 tablespoons balsamic vinegar
1 tablespoon agave nectar
½ tablespoon Dijon mustard
1 teaspoon fresh ginger, grated or minced
1 teaspoon toasted sesame oil
½ teaspoon black pepper
½ teaspoon salt

1. Toasting your walnuts? This step is not necessary but does intensify their taste. If you don't feel like it, just skip this step: Heat a dry (do not add oil) pan over medium heat. Add walnuts. After 1 minute, use a spatula to toss the walnuts. Toast for another minute, then toss again. Do this 3 or 4 times total for about 4 minutes of total time. Do not let the walnuts burn; they should be more fragrant and slightly darker in color. Remove from heat and set aside.
2. In a large mixing bowl add spring greens, microgreens, cranberries, walnuts, red onion, and feta. Gently stir to combine.
3. Add all dressing ingredients to a small mixing bowl and whisk together. Pour over salad and toss gently to evenly coat.
4. Plate the salad and top with pear slices; you can chop the pear and mix it in if you prefer, but it looks nice around the edges.

Party tip

You can prepare the dressing up to 5 days in advance and store it in an airtight container in the refrigerator.

WEDGE SALAD WITH BLUE CHEESE DRESSING

SERVES 4 TO 8

Bet you thought you couldn't have wedge salad if you are vegan. Think again. This salad hits just like the original. Perfect for holiday parties.

Dressing

1 cup vegan sour cream
½ cup vegan mayonnaise
1 tablespoon lemon juice
1 tablespoon nutritional yeast
½ teaspoon black pepper
½ teaspoon dried chives
½ teaspoon dried dill
½ teaspoon garlic powder
½ teaspoon onion powder
½ teaspoon salt
⅓ cup vegan feta crumbles (store-bought or pg. 40)

Salad

1 head iceberg lettuce, sliced into 4, 6, or 8 wedges*
1 cup cherry tomatoes, halved or quartered
½ cup red onion, chopped
3 ounces vegan bacon (*I use tempeh*), cooked according to package and chopped

1. Whisk all the dressing ingredients together, except for the feta or tofu.
2. Fold in the feta or tofu.
3. Cover the dressing and let it chill in the fridge while you prepare the salad.
4. Place lettuce wedges on serving platter. Top with blue cheese dressing. Add tomatoes, onion, and bacon pieces.

Note

*Cutting a head of lettuce for wedge salad can be intimidating, but it's actually easy. First, remove the outside layers that look wilted or loose. Wash the outside of the lettuce head and pat dry with a towel. Cut the lettuce in half, top to bottom. From here you can cut each half in half again to make 4 (or eventually 8) or cut each half into thirds for 6 portions. For 8, simply cut the ¼ pieces in half again. Lastly, using a sharp paring knife, trim the stems and remove any brown or tough core portions.

Party tip

Make the dressing the day before and store it in an airtight container in the refrigerator.

CAPRESE SALAD

SERVES 6 TO 8

Marinated tofu helps recreate this classic, refreshing dish. This dish is ideal for any occasion throughout the year.

1 block extra-firm tofu, drained and pressed
2 teaspoons apple cider vinegar
½ teaspoon salt
3 to 4 medium heirloom tomatoes (can sub any medium tomato)
16 large or 32 small fresh basil leaves
Balsamic glaze (about 2 tablespoons) for drizzling
Extra-virgin olive oil (about 2 tablespoons) for drizzling
Ground sea salt
Ground black pepper

1. Slice pressed tofu into 8 equal pieces, then slice those 8 in half, making 16 equal squares. Gently pat each tofu slice with a towel or paper towel to soak up any extra liquid.
2. Optional step: Round the edges of each square using a small cookie cutter or a knife. This is purely for aesthetic purposes.
3. Mix apple cider vinegar with salt in a small bowl or cup. With a spoon or a basting brush, coat both sides of the tofu pieces with the mixture and place on a plate or in a container. Set the tofu in the fridge to chill for at least 30 minutes, or overnight.
4. While tofu is chilling, slice the tomatoes into 16 thin slices and set aside.
5. Once tofu is finished chilling, assemble the platter. Place 1 tomato slice down on the dish. Next, place 1 large basil leaf or 2 small leaves on the tomato, followed by a slice of tofu. Continue this pattern until completed.
6. Drizzle the balsamic glaze and olive oil on top in a zig-zag manner and finish with cracked sea salt and black pepper.

Party tip

Marinate the tofu the night before your party and keep it in an airtight container in the refrigerator.

CREAMY CUCUMBER SALAD

SERVES 4 TO 6

This recipe is so simple and so delicious. My mom made this throughout the summer as a side dish to just about anything, though I could eat this as a main course because it's that good. Perfect to make ahead and really refreshing.

½ cup vegan mayonnaise
2 tablespoons balsamic vinegar
1 teaspoon garlic powder
1 teaspoon sesame oil
½ teaspoon ground sea salt
¼ teaspoon ground pepper
6 mini cucumbers, thinly sliced

1. Whisk together the mayonnaise, vinegar, garlic powder, sesame oil, salt, and pepper.
2. Add the cucumber slices and gently toss to evenly coat.
3. Chill in the refrigerator for at least an hour before serving.

Party tip

Make this the day before and store it in the refrigerator in an airtight container.

THE BEST POTATO SALAD

SERVES 12 TO 16

This is the best potato salad.

- 5 pounds red potatoes or Yukon Gold potatoes, chopped into bite-size chunks about ¾ - inch, skin on or off depending on your preference
- 1 ½ cup vegan mayo
- ⅓ cup fresh dill, finely chopped
- ¼ cup yellow mustard
- ½ teaspoon celery salt
- ½ teaspoon garlic powder
- ½ teaspoon ground black pepper
- ½ teaspoon salt
- 1 cup celery, finely chopped
- 1 cup dill pickles, finely chopped
- 1 cup red onion, finely chopped

1. Add potatoes to a large pot and cover with 1 ½ inches of water.
2. Heat on medium-high until water comes to a boil.
3. Reduce to a simmer and cook until potatoes are fork-tender but still firm, approximately 10 to 15 minutes. Be careful not to overcook them.
4. Drain potatoes and set aside to cool. I recommend lining a baking sheet with aluminum foil and spreading the potatoes out so they can cool quicker and evenly.
5. Add mayo, dill, yellow mustard, celery salt, garlic powder, black pepper, and salt to a mixing bowl and mix everything together until evenly combined.
6. In a large bowl, combine the potatoes with the onions, pickles, and celery.
7. Pour in the dressing and stir until evenly coated. Refrigerate overnight or for at least 2 hours before serving.

Party Tip

Potato salad tastes even better on day 2! Make this the day before and keep it covered in the refrigerator.

GRILLED MUSHROOMS SKEWERS

MAKES 10 TO 12 SKEWERS

These mushrooms are savory, tender, and meaty. Seasoned with balsamic vinegar, garlic, and spices and grilled to perfection.

¼ cup balsamic vinegar
¼ cup olive oil
2 tablespoons soy sauce (can sub tamari or coconut aminos)
2 garlic cloves, minced
1 tablespoon Dijon mustard
½ teaspoon black pepper
½ teaspoon garlic powder
½ teaspoon onion powder
½ teaspoon salt
1 ½ pounds (24 oz) cremini or button mushrooms, halved
12 skewers

Garnish (optional)
Fresh parsley, chopped

1. Add the balsamic vinegar, olive oil, soy sauce, garlic, mustard, salt, pepper, garlic powder, and onion powder to a mixing bowl and whisk together until evenly combined.
2. Add the mushrooms to the dressing and toss until all the mushrooms are coated.
3. Cover and let marinate in the refrigerator for 1 to 4 hours.
4. Preheat the grill to medium-high heat (or 375°F). If you are using wooden skewers, soak the skewers in water for 30 minutes prior to grilling.
5. Thread the mushrooms onto the skewers.
6. Place the skewers on the grill and cook for 10 minutes, turning them occasionally. Mushrooms are done when they are lightly charred and tender.
7. Serve on a platter with a sprinkle of fresh parsley (optional).

GRILLED VEGGIE KABOBS

MAKES 8 TO 10 KABOBS

Colorful veggies marinated in a flavorful blend of garlic and herbs. The perfect side dish! Being healthy never tasted this good.

Marinade

⅓ cup extra-virgin olive oil
Juice from 1 lemon (or 3 tablespoons)
2 garlic cloves, minced or pressed
½ teaspoon black pepper
½ teaspoon dried basil
½ teaspoon dried oregano
½ teaspoon dried parsley
½ teaspoon salt

Veggie kabobs

2 red bell peppers, cut into bite-sized pieces
2 zucchini, sliced into bite-sized pieces
1 red onion, cut into chunks
8 ounces button mushrooms, halved
8 to 10 wooden or metal skewers

1. Mix the marinade ingredients in a large Ziploc bag or bowl.
2. Add the peppers, zucchini, onion, and mushrooms to the marinade and allow to chill in the refrigerator for 2 hours up to overnight. Give them a shake or stir occasionally.
3. Preheat grill to medium-high heat (or 375°F). If you are using wooden skewers, soak them in water for at least 30 minutes to ensure they do not burn when grilling.
4. Thread the vegetables onto skewers in whichever order or pattern you prefer.
5. Grill for about 10 minutes, carefully turning skewers every 3 minutes, until tender with charred edges.

Party tip

Marinate the veggies the night before and keep them in the refrigerator in an airtight container.

BRUSCHETTA PASTA

SERVES 6 TO 8

With fresh tomatoes, basil, savory oil, and a trio of vinegars for a sweet tanginess, this pasta dish is my go-to when hosting.

1 box (1 pound) short pasta of choice (I like to use farfalle).
1 pint cherry or grape tomatoes (10 to 12 ounces), halved or sliced
1 cup red onion (about ½ onion), diced
½ cup fresh basil, chopped
½ cup extra-virgin olive oil
2 tablespoons balsamic glaze
2 tablespoons balsamic vinegar
2 tablespoons red wine vinegar
1 teaspoon sea salt
½ teaspoon black pepper
½ teaspoon garlic powder

Garnish (optional)

1 cup vegan croutons, crushed
¼ cup vegan parmesan, grated

1. Cook the pasta according to the directions on the package until al dente. Drain pasta.
2. Combine the pasta, tomatoes, red onions, and basil in a large mixing bowl.
3. In a separate bowl or jar, make the dressing by whisking together the olive oil, balsamic glaze, balsamic vinegar, red wine vinegar, salt, pepper, and garlic powder.
4. Pour dressing over pasta and gently toss until evenly coated.
5. Cover and chill in the refrigerator for at least 1 hour. Garnish with crushed croutons and parmesan just before serving.

Party Tip

Make this pasta salad, without the basil or croutons, 1 or 2 days in advance of your party and store it, covered, in the refrigerator. Add the basil the day of the party and the croutons when you are serving.

IMITATION CRABLESS PASTA SALAD

SERVES 6 TO 8

I used to make imitation crab pasta salad for our family gatherings on the Chester River in Maryland. It's a really simple recipe that has so much flavor. Now, shredded tofu takes the place of imitation crab. Pairs perfectly with a sunny day and a beer!

16-ounce package medium shell pasta (or short pasta of your choice)
14 to 16 ounces super-firm tofu, drained and pressed (can sub extra-firm)
1 cup celery, finely chopped
1 ¼ cup vegan mayonnaise
3 ½ teaspoons Old Bay seasoning
½ teaspoon celery salt
½ teaspoon garlic powder
¼ teaspoon black pepper

1. Cook pasta according to package directions, drain, and set aside to cool.
2. Shred tofu with the large grate on a cheese grater into a large mixing bowl.
3. Add the pasta and the celery to the tofu and gently mix until they are evenly mixed.
4. In a separate small mixing bowl, stir together the mayo, Old Bay, celery salt, garlic powder, and black pepper.
5. Add the mayo dressing to the large mixing bowl and gently stir until the pasta, tofu, and celery are evenly coated.
6. Chill in the refrigerator for at least 1 hour before serving.

Note
Mix the tofu gently to not break all the shreds. This is solely for the appearance of the dish, so it resembles shredded crabstick. If you find that your shreds are mostly broken, don't panic, it will still taste amazing.

Party tip
This pasta salad tastes even better the next day; make it in advance and store it in an airtight container in the refrigerator.

HOAGIE PASTA SALAD

SERVES 6 TO 8

Sub, hero, hoagie, whatever you call them, they're delicious! This pasta dish delivers you those distinctive flavors in a bowl. With the tangy oil and vinegar, Italian herbs and seasonings, and the fresh crunch of the veggies, this is the ultimate crowd-pleasing pasta!

16-ounce package of your favorite short pasta (like farfalle, penne, or rotini)
1 ½ cups cherry tomatoes, quartered
1 ½ cups cucumber, chopped
1 cup banana peppers (jarred), chopped
1 cup red onion, chopped
1 cup vegan ham slices, chopped*
1 cup vegan cheese slices, chopped*
½ cup vegan mayonnaise
⅓ cup extra-virgin olive oil
¼ cup red wine vinegar
1 ½ teaspoons dried oregano
1 teaspoon Dijon mustard
1 teaspoon dried thyme
½ teaspoon black pepper
½ teaspoon dried basil
½ teaspoon salt

1. Cook pasta according to package, drain, and add to a large bowl.
2. Add the tomatoes, cucumber, banana peppers, red onion, vegan meat, and cheese to the pasta.
3. In a separate small mixing bowl, whisk together the mayo, olive oil, vinegar, oregano, mustard, thyme, pepper, basil, and salt.
4. Pour the dressing over the pasta and veggies and gently toss until it is mixed evenly and coated. Chill in the refrigerator for at least 1 hour before serving.

Note

*This recipe uses store-bought vegan meat and cheese. I like to use vegan ham slices and vegan provolone cheese, but depending on what stores you have access to, you can use vegan pepperoni, turkey, etc., or omit the vegan meat part altogether; it will still taste delicious. Likewise, if you cannot find a vegan provolone, cheddar or American will also work.

Party tip

This is the perfect make-ahead pasta salad, as the flavor gets better overnight. Make it the day before and store it, covered, in the refrigerator.

DIPS

FRUIT DIP

SERVES 6 TO 8

Vegan version of the oh-so-sweet and creamy dip. Strawberries alone are just strawberries. Strawberries with fruit dip, that's a party!

8 ounces vegan cream cheese, softened
½ cup powdered sugar
1 teaspoon lemon juice
1 teaspoon vanilla extract

1. Add all ingredients to a mixing bowl and blend with an electric mixer until evenly combined and smooth.
2. Serve with an assortment of dippers like fresh fruit, soft pretzels, and vegan cookies.

Party tip

This dip can be made up to 3 days before your party and stored in an airtight container in the refrigerator. Let it sit out on the counter for 20 minutes to soften and give it a god stir before serving.

STRAWBERRY JALAPEÑO SALSA

SERVES 8 TO 10

Fresh and vibrant combination of sweet strawberries and a spicy kick from onions and jalapeño.

1 pint fresh strawberries, diced
½ cup red onion, finely chopped
1 jalapeño, seeded and finely chopped
⅓ cup fresh cilantro, finely chopped
Juice from 1 lime (about 2 tablespoons)
¼ teaspoon chili powder
¼ teaspoon ground sea salt
¼ teaspoon sugar

1. Combine all ingredients in a bowl, stir until evenly combined. Done!

CANTINA SALSA

SERVES 8 TO 10

This salsa is so easy and packed with so much more flavor than store-bought. Grab the chips and pour the margaritas!

14.5-ounce can diced tomatoes
½ cup white onion, roughly chopped
⅓ cup fresh cilantro
1 jalapeño, seeded
Juice of 1 lime (or 2 tablespoons)
2 garlic cloves, peeled
½ teaspoon cumin
½ teaspoon salt

1. Add all ingredients to a blender or food processor, blend or pulse until smooth and sauce-like. Done!

Party tip
Make this salsa up to 4 days ahead of your party and keep it in an airtight container in the refrigerator.

NO-CATCH CEVICHE

SERVES 6 TO 8

Hearts of palm take the place of seafood in this classic dish. Filled with fresh and vibrant veggies and fruits, it's light and yet very satisfying. Perfect for a hot summer day with a Paloma or Prosecco!

14-ounce can hearts of palm, chopped
¾ cup grape or cherry tomatoes, halved or quartered
¾ cup cucumber, diced
½ cup red onion, diced
1 jalapeño, seeded and finely chopped
¾ cup fresh lime juice (about 4 limes)
⅓ cup fresh cilantro, chopped
2 garlic cloves, pressed
1 tablespoon extra-virgin olive oil
2 teaspoons kosher salt
½ teaspoon black pepper
1 nori seaweed sheet, very finely diced or cut (optional)*
1 semi-firm avocado, diced

1. Add hearts of palm, tomatoes, cucumber, red onion, and jalapeños to a bowl.
2. In a separate bowl, whisk together the lime juice, cilantro, garlic, olive oil, salt, pepper, and nori sheet if you are using it.
3. Pour the marinade into the large bowl and gently stir to coat everything.
4. Cover and chill in the fridge for at least 30 minutes, preferably 1 to 2 hours, before serving.
5. When you are ready to serve, add the diced avocado and gently stir to combine. Transfer to your serving dish and enjoy!

Note

*Not familiar with a nori sheet? I got you. Nori sheets are dried seaweed. They are used often in sushi rolls. They appear in vegan recipes often to give a seafood flavor. If you want the ceviche to taste like there is seafood in it, add one of these! If that's not important to you, then feel free to omit. This ceviche tastes amazing with or without it. It's very flavorful and refreshing on its own.

If you want to give it a try, here is a tip to cut it. I suggest cutting the sheet into long strips. Stack the strips and finely chop them. You can also use kitchen scissors.

SPICY GUACAMOLE

SERVES 6 TO 8

Guac, salsa, chips, and margaritas. The perfect party menu! This guacamole has a bit of a kick. Pair it with one of my salsas and get the party started!

4 ripe avocados
¼ cup cherry tomatoes, finely chopped
¼ cup fire-roasted corn, drained (can sub sweet whole kernel corn)
¼ cup fresh cilantro, finely chopped
¼ cup jalapeño, finely chopped
¼ cup red onion, finely chopped
½ teaspoon chili powder
½ teaspoon salt or to taste
Juice from 1 lime

Garnish (optional)
Handful of fire-roasted corn
Sprinkle of chili powder

1. Slice the avocados in half, remove the pit, and scoop out the flesh into a medium-sized mixing bowl.
2. Mash the avocado with a fork until you've reached your preferred consistency.
3. Add the remainder of the ingredients and mix until evenly combined.
4. Give it a taste and add more salt if necessary.
5. Scoop into a serving dish and top with a light sprinkle of chili powder and a handful of corn.

Party Tip
If you want to make this the morning of your party, store it in a container with a piece of plastic wrap on top of the guacamole. You want the plastic wrap to be touching the dip so as not to allow any air. Then cover it again with either more plastic wrap or a lid. There may still be a little browning that occurs, but you can scrape that off.

AVOCADO SWEET PEA HUMMUS

SERVES 6 TO 8

Avocado and peas are the perfect combination of sweetness, balanced with the refreshing taste of dill. Add this hummus to your next spring or summer gathering!

15 ounces canned chickpeas, drained and rinsed
1 cup frozen sweet peas, thawed or lightly steamed, divided
2 medium ripe avocados, pitted and peeled
2 tablespoons extra-virgin olive oil
1 ½ tablespoons tahini
Juice from 1 lemon (about 3 tablespoons)
1 clove garlic, peeled
1 teaspoon salt
½ teaspoon black pepper
¼ cup fresh dill, roughly chopped

Garnish (optional)

1 to 2 tablespoons extra-virgin olive oil
½ to 1 tablespoon fresh dill, finely chopped

1. Add chickpeas, ½ cup of the sweet peas (set aside the rest), and the remaining ingredients to a food processor or high-speed blender.
2. Blend for several minutes until creamy and smooth. If the hummus is too thick, add 1 tablespoon of warm water and continue to blend. Repeat the last step as many times as needed until the desired consistency.
3. Transfer to a serving dish and top with ½ cup of sweet peas, a drizzle of olive oil, and extra dill.

Party tip

Because there is avocado in this hummus, you do have to worry about a slight change in color if made too far in advance. I recommend making this only a few hours before and covering it with plastic wrap. Make sure the plastic wrap touches the surface of the hummus so as not to allow air to get in. Garnish when you are ready to serve.

DILL PICKLE HUMMUS

SERVES 8 TO 10

If you love dill pickles as much as I do, this hummus is a must! Creamy chickpeas paired with the distinct tangy, herby flavor of dill pickles.

2 15-ounce cans chickpeas, drained and rinsed
½ cup tahini
¼ cup extra-virgin olive oil
¼ cup fresh dill
4 tablespoons dill pickle brine
Juice from 1 lemon (about 2 tablespoons)
1 clove garlic, peeled
½ teaspoon salt
¼ teaspoon black pepper

Garnish (optional)
2 to 3 mini dill pickles, diced
½ tablespoon fresh dill, finely chopped

1. Add the hummus ingredients to a high-speed blender or food processor. Blend until very smooth.
2. If hummus is too thick for your liking, add a tablespoon of water *(or more dill pickle brine if you're as obsessed as I am!)* and continue to blend. Repeat until you reach your desired consistency.
3. Transfer to your serving dish and garnish with dill and chopped pickles.

Party tip
Make this hummus up to 3 days in advance of your party and store it in an airtight container in the refrigerator. Garnish just before serving.

BEER CHEESE

SERVES 6 TO 8

The ultimate creamy, cheesy dip with hints of beer and spices. You may as well make a double batch and keep some for yourself, because this dish will be the first one to go. Pairs perfectly with soft pretzels and cold beer!

¼ cup vegan butter
¼ cup flour
1 cup non-dairy milk
1 cup lager-style beer
2 tablespoons nutritional yeast
1 tablespoon spicy mustard
1 teaspoon garlic powder
1 teaspoon Tabasco sauce (sub your favorite vinegar-based hot sauce)
1 teaspoon vegan Worcestershire sauce
½ teaspoon black pepper
½ teaspoon salt
½ teaspoon smoked paprika
1 ½ cups vegan shredded cheddar cheese

1. Heat butter in a medium saucepan on medium-high heat.
2. Once melted, add flour and whisk until combined into a paste.
3. Add milk and continue whisking until smooth.
4. Add beer, nutritional yeast, mustard, garlic, Tabasco, Worcestershire, pepper, salt, and smoked paprika. Continue to heat, stirring, until the sauce begins to simmer and thicken.
5. Turn heat down to low. Add cheddar cheese and continue to stir until the cheese has melted and combined evenly. Transfer to your serving dish and dig in!

Party tip

Beer cheese can be made the day before and stored in an airtight container in the refrigerator. Reheat on the stove over medium-low heat, stirring constantly, until the cheese is the desired temperature. If it is too thick, add a splash of non-dairy milk.

GUINNESS ONION DIP

SERVES 8 TO 10

Guinness takes this classic to a new level. The onions are soaked in the delicious stout for a day and then caramelized to perfection.

1 yellow onion, sliced
1 white onion, sliced
2 14.9-ounce cans of Guinness draught stout
4 tablespoons vegan butter
1 teaspoon salt
3 garlic cloves, finely minced
8 ounces vegan cream cheese, softened
1 cup vegan sour cream
½ teaspoon black pepper
½ teaspoon garlic powder
½ teaspoon onion powder

Garnish (optional)
1 tablespoon fresh chives, chopped

1. Place onions in a large sealable container. Pour Guinness over onion slices until covered. Cover the container tightly and refrigerate overnight, preferably for 24 hours.
2. After 24 hours, scoop or pour ¼ cup of the Guinness from the onion container into a measuring cup and set aside. Drain the onions.
3. Add butter to a large frying pan and melt on medium-low heat. Add the onions and salt. Let the onions slowly caramelize for about 30 minutes, stirring occasionally.
4. Add garlic and sauté for 1 more minute, stirring frequently.
5. Add the ¼ cup of Guinness that was set aside to the frying pan along with the pepper, garlic powder, and onion powder. Turn heat up to medium-high and simmer until Guinness has evaporated, about 5 minutes. Remove pan from heat and set aside.
6. In a food processor or blender, add cream cheese and sour cream and blend on low until smooth and creamy. Add onions to food and pulse until evenly combined and the onions are the desired size (*I like the onions to still be fairly large pieces, approximately ½ inch).*
7. Chill in the refrigerator, covered, for at least 1 to 2 hours before serving. Garnish with chopped chives.

Party tip
This dip tastes even better on day 2 or 3, so feel free to make it in advance. Make sure to still give the onions 24 hours in the Guinness—it really does take it to the next level!

BEAN DIP

SERVES 8 TO 10

This might be the best bean dip you have ever had. Yes, it takes more time than buying store-bought, but you can do most of the work in advance, and it's going to wow your guests. Perfect for game day!

3 tablespoons vegan butter
½ small white onion (about ½ cup), diced
3 garlic cloves, minced or pressed
2 14.5-ounce cans of pinto beans, drained and rinsed
½ cup enchilada sauce
4-ounce can diced green chiles, drained (mild or hot depending on your spice level preference)
½ teaspoon black pepper
½ teaspoon chili powder
½ teaspoon cumin
½ teaspoon paprika
½ teaspoon salt
1 cup vegan shredded cheddar cheese, divided
¼ cup vegan sour cream

Garnish (optional)

1 Roma tomato, diced
½ small white onion (about ½ cup), diced
1 avocado, chopped
1 to 2 tablespoons fresh cilantro, chopped
¼ cup vegan feta cheese crumbles (store-bought or pg. 40)
1 to 2 tablespoons green onions, chopped

1. Preheat oven to 375°F.
2. In a large frying pan, heat butter on medium heat. Add onions and cook, stirring frequently, until onions become translucent, about 5 to 7 minutes.
3. Add garlic and cook another 30 seconds, stirring frequently.
4. Add beans, enchilada sauce, green chiles, black pepper, chili powder, cumin, paprika, and salt. Simmer for 3 to 4 minutes, stirring occasionally. Remove from heat.
5. Transfer bean mixture to a food processor or blender. If your food processor cannot handle hot food, allow the mixture to cool first. Use the pulse setting to mash the bean mixture until you get a refried bean texture of your liking.
6. Transfer the bean mixture to a mixing bowl and fold in ½ cup of the cheese and the sour cream.
7. Evenly spread the mixture into a 9x9-inch (or similar size) baking dish. Top with the remaining ½ cup cheddar cheese.
8. Bake uncovered for 20 to 25 minutes or until the cheese on top is melted. Let cool for 10 to 15 minutes before serving. Serve as is or top with any of the above garnish ingredients.

Party tip

Make the beans ahead and store them in the refrigerator, in an airtight container, until you are ready to serve. When you are ready, just mix in the cheese, top with cheese, and bake.

STREET CORN DIP

SERVES 6 TO 8

Rich and cheesy and packed with flavor!

- 1 cup shredded vegan cheese (Mexican blend, cheddar, or mozzarella), divided
- 8 ounces vegan cream cheese, softened
- ½ cup vegan sour cream
- 2 tablespoons hot sauce *(I use Cholula Original)*
- Juice from ½ lime (or 1 tablespoon)
- 2 garlic cloves, finely minced or pressed
- 30-ounce can of corn, drained and rinsed, handful set aside for garnish
- 2 jalapeño peppers, deseeded and chopped
- ½ cup fresh cilantro, chopped, plus 2 tablespoons set aside for garnish
- ½ cup red onion, finely chopped, plus 2 tablespoons set aside for garnish

Garnish (optional)

4 ounces vegan feta crumbles (store-bought or pg. 40)

1. Preheat oven to 350°F and spray a 9x13-inch baking dish (or similar size) with a nonstick cooking spray and set aside.
2. Combine ½ cup shredded cheese, cream cheese, sour cream, hot sauce, lime juice, and garlic in a bowl and mix with a spoon or electric mixer until evenly combined.
3. Stir in the remaining ingredients: corn, jalapeno, cilantro, and onion.
4. Top with ½ cup of shredded cheese. Bake uncovered for 20 to 25 minutes, or until cheese is melted on top.
5. Let stand for 10 to 15 minutes before serving. Garnish with some extra corn, cilantro, onion, and vegan feta (optional).

Party tip

Assemble this dip the day before your party and store it in an airtight container in the refrigerator. Let the dip sit on the counter for about 30 minutes to come to room temperature and then bake.

7-LAYER DIP

SERVES 8 TO 12

Tailgates, parties, or potlucks, the 7-layer dip is perfect for any occasion. Savory refried beans are the star of the dish, paired with creamy guacamole and sour cream, and topped with crunchy fresh vegetables and vegan cheese; this is the ultimate flavor experience!

Layer 1: Refried beans (OR 16-ounce can of vegan refried beans)
2 tablespoons olive oil
1 medium yellow onion, diced
2 garlic cloves, minced
15-ounce can black beans, drained but keep liquid
⅓ cup liquid from bean can (can also use water)
Juice from ½ lime (1 tablespoon)
1 teaspoon chili powder
1 teaspoon cumin
1 teaspoon paprika
½ teaspoon dried oregano
½ teaspoon pepper
½ teaspoon salt

Layer 2: Guacamole (OR 2 cups of store-bought guacamole)
4 medium ripe avocados
¼ cup fresh cilantro, finely chopped
1 jalapeño, deseeded and finely chopped
Juice from 1 lime (2 tablespoons)
½ teaspoon garlic powder
½ teaspoon onion powder
½ teaspoon salt

1. Layer 1 is the beans. *If you are making them, continue with this step. if you can't be bothered with that today and want to get straight to the eating and partying, open the can of refried beans and* ***skip to step 5***. Heat olive oil in a pan on medium-high heat. Add onions and sauté, stirring frequently until onions are translucent, approximately 5 to 7 minutes.
2. Add garlic and continue to cook for another 30 seconds, keep stirring so the garlic doesn't burn.
3. Stir in the beans, the bean liquid (or water), lime juice, chili powder, cumin, paprika, oregano, pepper, and salt. Reduce heat to medium and cook another 2 minutes, stirring frequently.
4. The last step for the beans is to get the consistency you want. Use a food processor, potato masher, or immersion blender to pulse, mash, or blend it down until you reach the refried bean texture you prefer. *I like mine to be slightly chunky.*
5. Spread the beans evenly in an 8x8-inch casserole dish (or similar size).
6. Mash the avocados in a medium bowl using a potato masher or fork until you get the guacamole consistency you prefer. *OR open your store-bought guacamole and* ***skip to step 8***.
7. Stir in the cilantro, jalapeño, lime juice, garlic powder, onion powder, and salt.
8. Spread the guacamole evenly on top of the beans.

recipe and ingredients continue

recipe continued from previous page

Remaining layers

1 ½ cups vegan sour cream
½ cup your favorite salsa
2 cups shredded iceberg lettuce
1 ½ cups shredded vegan cheddar cheese
¾ cup cherry or grape tomatoes, quartered or halved
2.25-ounce can of sliced black olives, drained
1 jalapeño, deseeded and sliced
¼ cup green onions, chopped

9. In a small bowl, stir together the sour cream and the salsa and spread this evenly on top of the guacamole.
10. Sprinkle the lettuce evenly on top of the sour cream and salsa.
11. Sprinkle the cheese on top of the lettuce.
12. Top with tomatoes, olives, jalapeños, and green onions and dig in!

Party tip

This dish contains lots of veggies that can wilt and avocado that can brown, so I recommend assembling it the day of your party or the night before and storing it, covered, in the refrigerator. The beans can be made up to 4 days in advance of your party and stored in the refrigerator in an airtight container.

SPINACH AND ARTICHOKE DIP

SERVES 6 TO 8

A vegan version of a classic dish. Artichokes and spinach smothered in a creamy cheese blend.

1 14-ounce can artichoke hearts in water, drained and chopped
1 ½ cup frozen chopped spinach, thawed and drained
8 ounces vegan cream cheese, softened
½ cup grated vegan parmesan cheese
½ cup shredded vegan mozzarella cheese
¼ cup vegan mayonnaise
2 cloves garlic, minced or pressed
½ teaspoon black pepper
½ teaspoon dried basil
½ teaspoon salt

1. Preheat oven to 350°F. Spray a small baking dish with nonstick cooking spray and set aside.
2. Combine the artichokes and spinach in a bowl and set aside.
3. In a separate bowl, mix cream cheese, parmesan cheese, ¼ cup of the mozzarella cheese, mayonnaise, garlic, pepper, basil, and salt until evenly combined using a spoon or electric mixer.
4. Gently fold the artichokes and spinach in with the cream cheese mixture.
5. Transfer dip to the baking dish and top with the remaining ¼ cup mozzarella cheese. Bake uncovered for about 25 minutes, until the cheese on top is melted. Let cool for 10 to 15 minutes before serving.

Party tip

You can make this dip a day or 2 before baking. Cover it tightly and store it in the refrigerator. Take the dip out for about 30 minutes before baking.

BUFFALO TOFU DIP

SERVES 8 TO 10

Creamy, rich, spicy, and meaty. The tofu is baked ahead and seasoned to perfection to give a real meaty texture and taste in this twist on a classic appetizer.

Tofu "chicken"

1 block extra-firm tofu (14 to 16 ounces), drained and pressed
⅓ cup nutritional yeast
1 teaspoon garlic powder
1 teaspoon onion powder
½ teaspoon black pepper
½ teaspoon salt

Dip

8 ounces vegan cream cheese, softened
½ cup Frank's RedHot Sauce (or hot sauce of choice)
¼ cup vegan mayonnaise
¾ cup vegan shredded cheddar cheese
1 teaspoon garlic powder
1 teaspoon onion powder
½ teaspoon black pepper
½ teaspoon salt

1. Preheat oven to 350°F and line a baking sheet with parchment paper.
2. Cut the tofu into small cubes, about ½ to ¾-inch thick cubes.
3. In a medium bowl, combine the nutritional yeast, garlic powder, onion powder, pepper, and salt.
4. Add the tofu to the bowl. Toss or cover and shake gently until all the tofu is coated with the seasoning.
5. Bake for 35 minutes. Set aside to cool when done and keep the oven at 350°F.
6. In a large mixing bowl, add softened cream cheese, hot sauce, and mayonnaise. Mix until evenly combined. Add cheese, garlic powder, onion powder, pepper, and salt, and stir again until thoroughly mixed.
7. Fold in the tofu.
8. Transfer mixture to baking dish and bake uncovered for 25 minutes.

Party tip

You can prepare the dip the day before and store it in the refrigerator, unbaked and covered. Allow to sit on the counter for about 20 to 30 minutes before baking.

PIEROGI DIP

SERVES 6 TO 8

Pierogi are my favorite food. My second favorite is pierogi dip. This dish combines all the savory, comforting, nostalgic flavors of classic potato and cheddar pierogi into a creamy, mouthwatering dip. Serve with sliced baguette, crackers, pretzels, or just by the spoonful—it's really that good!

2 pounds russet or Yukon Gold potatoes, peeled and cut into approximately 2-inch pieces
3 tablespoons vegan butter, divided
½ cup yellow onion, finely chopped
½ teaspoon salt
¼ teaspoon pepper
3 tablespoons non-dairy milk
¼ cup vegan cream cheese, softened
¼ cup vegan sour cream
1⅓ cup shredded vegan cheddar cheese, divided

Party tip

You can prepare the dip the day before and store it in the refrigerator, unbaked and covered. Allow to sit on the counter for about 20 to 30 minutes before baking.

1. Place potatoes in a pot and add water until potatoes are covered by an inch. Heat on high and bring to a boil.
2. Reduce the heat to medium-low, and simmer, uncovered, for 15 to 20 minutes, or until you can easily pierce the potato with a fork. *If you're good at multitasking, start the onions while the potatoes are cooking.* When potatoes are done cooking, drain well in a colander and add potatoes to a large mixing bowl.
3. Melt 1 tablespoon of vegan butter in a pan over medium heat. Add the onions and sauté, stirring frequently, until tender and starting to brown, about 6 to 8 minutes.
4. Add the salt and pepper and cook for 1 more minute. Remove from heat.
5. Preheat oven to 375°F.
6. Start to mash the potatoes with a potato masher in the mixing bowl. When they are mostly mashed, add the remaining 2 tablespoons of butter and the milk and continue to mash with the potato masher or an electric hand mixer until you have a smooth mashed potato consistency.
7. In a separate bowl, add the softened cream cheese and whip using an electric hand mixer (or stand mixer). When it is smooth, add the sour cream and mix again just until it is evenly combined.
8. Now add the cream mixture and the onions to the potatoes and gently stir to combine.
9. Lastly, fold in 1 cup of the vegan cheese.
10. Spread evenly into a baking dish and top with the remaining ⅓ cup of cheese.
11. Bake uncovered for 20 to 25 minutes, until the cheese on top melts. Let cool for 10 to 15 minutes before serving.

HORS D'OEUVRES

SPICED EDAMAME

SERVES 4 TO 6

Need a dish on the lighter side to balance out the menu? This edamame is perfectly spiced, packing a major flavor punch, while also being light and healthy.

- 12-ounce package of frozen edamame in their pods
- 2 tablespoons soy sauce (can sub tamari or coconut aminos)
- 1 tablespoon toasted sesame oil
- ¼ teaspoon black pepper
- ¼ teaspoon crushed red pepper flakes (optional if you like heat)
- ¼ teaspoon garlic powder
- ¼ teaspoon kosher salt
- ¼ teaspoon onion powder
- 1 ½ tablespoons vegetable oil
- 1 garlic clove, finely minced

1. Cook edamame. To boil them, bring a medium pot of water to boil and add a pinch of salt. Add edamame and boil until pods are tender and bright green, about 5 minutes. Drain and pat dry.
To microwave them, add them to a microwave-safe dish along with ⅓ cup water and a pinch of salt. Partially cover the dish and microwave on high until pods are tender and a bright green, approximately 3 to 5 minutes depending on your microwave. Drain and pat dry.
If your frozen edamame can be steamed in the bag, follow the directions on the packaging. Drain and pat dry.
2. Whisk together soy sauce, toasted sesame oil, black pepper, crushed red pepper, garlic powder, salt, and onion powder in a bowl and set aside.
3. Add vegetable oil to a large pan and heat on medium heat. Add edamame and pan-fry for about 4 to 5 minutes, stirring occasionally, until pods begin to crisp.
4. Add garlic and cook another minute, stirring frequently so the garlic does not burn.
5. Reduce heat to low and add sauce mixture. Stir until all the pods are coated in the sauce.
6. Transfer the edamame to a serving dish and enjoy!

Party tip

This dish is delicious hot, at room temperature, or cold, so if you want to make this in advance, store it in an airtight container up to 3 days before your party. You can serve it right out of the refrigerator or reheat it in the microwave on 30-second intervals until you reach the temperature you want.

LETTUCE WRAPS

SERVES 6 TO 8

Lettuce wraps are a great addition to any party menu. They're easy to make and serve, and guests love making their own wraps. These are fresh and light with an umami-rich tofu filling.

2 tablespoons soy sauce (can sub coconut aminos or tamari)
2 tablespoons hoisin sauce
½ tablespoon chili oil
½ tablespoon sesame oil
1 tablespoon agave nectar
1 tablespoon peanut butter
1 tablespoon rice vinegar
2 teaspoons sweet chili sauce
½ teaspoon garlic powder
¼ teaspoon onion powder
¼ teaspoon powdered ginger
2 tablespoons vegetable oil, divided
14.5- to 16-ounce package of extra-firm tofu, drained and pressed
½ yellow onion, finely diced
1 red bell pepper, diced
8-ounce can water chestnuts, drained and diced
2 cloves garlic, minced or pressed
2 small heads of Bibb lettuce, leaves separated (or whichever lettuce you prefer)

Garnish (optional)

½ cup shredded carrots
¼ cup cashews or peanuts, crushed or roughly chopped
¼ cup green onions, sliced

1. In a small mixing bowl, whisk together the soy sauce, hoisin sauce, chili oil, sesame oil, agave nectar, peanut butter, rice vinegar, sweet chili sauce, garlic powder, onion powder, and powdered ginger until thoroughly combined. Set aside.
2. Heat 1 tablespoon of vegetable oil in a pan on medium-high heat.
3. Crumble tofu into pan or break into big pieces and use your spatula to break into smaller crumbles until it resembles ground meat. Cook until tofu begins to brown, stirring occasionally, approximately 7 to 10 minutes. Transfer the tofu to a clean plate or bowl.
4. Heat the remaining 1 tablespoon of vegetable oil in the same pan on medium-high heat.
5. Add onions and cook until translucent and tender, about 5 to 7 minutes.
6. Stir in bell pepper, water chestnuts, and garlic and reduce heat to medium. Continue to cook for another 5 minutes, until the peppers are tender.
7. Stir in the sauce and turn down the heat to low. Simmer for 2 minutes to allow the flavors to combine.
8. Transfer filling to a serving dish and serve alongside lettuce leaves and garnishes. Alternatively, you can divide the filling amongst the lettuce and top with garnishes, but this may lead to the lettuce wilting if not consumed immediately.

Party tip

Make the lettuce wrap filling up to 2 days before your party and keep it in an airtight container in the refrigerator. Reheat in a pan on medium heat with 1 tablespoon oil for about 3 to 5 minutes or in the microwave in 30 to 60 second intervals, stirring each time, until desired temperature is reached. Prep the lettuce the night before and store them in an airtight container, with a paper towel, in the refrigerator.

SUSHI WITH SPICY CRABLESS STICK AND TOMATO TUNA

MAKES 6 ROLLS

This isn't your average veggie roll. This one is from the specialty roll menu. The shredded tofu 'crabstick' and tomato 'tuna' taste just like their seafood counterparts. Add one or both to your rolls and top with the decadent eel sauce.

Sushi roll

1 block of extra-firm tofu, drained, pressed, and sliced into 8 to 10 long strips
¼ cup soy sauce
1 tablespoon hoisin sauce
2 garlic cloves, finely minced or pressed
½ tablespoon cornstarch
1 tablespoon sesame oil (can sub extra virgin olive oil)
2 cups uncooked sushi rice
¼ cup seasoned rice vinegar (sushi vinegar)
2 avocados, pitted and thinly sliced
2 Persian (mini) cucumbers, thinly sliced
3 medium jalapeños, thinly sliced lengthwise
6 nori sheets

Eel sauce

⅓ cup soy sauce
¼ cup maple syrup
3 tablespoons rice vinegar
2 teaspoons cornstarch

Sushi rolls

1. Add the tofu to a bowl or container.
2. Whisk together the soy sauce, hoisin, and garlic and pour over the tofu slices. Flip the tofu around until all sides are covered. Marinate for at least 30 minutes. If you are good at multitasking, make the rice while the tofu is marinating.
3. Remove the tofu from the marinade and place on a plate or in a bowl. Sprinkle cornstarch and gently toss until tofu is coated.
4. Heat sesame oil in a pan over high heat. Add tofu strips and cook untouched until browned, about 2 to 4 minutes. Flip tofu and continue to cook, flipping occasionally, until browned on all sides. Remove from heat and set aside.
5. Cook rice according to package.
6. Once the rice has finished cooking, pour the vinegar over the rice and gently toss until evenly coated. Make sure not to mash the rice. Set aside.
7. Place a nori sheet, shiny side down, on a bamboo sushi mat*. Set up your sushi station with your sushi rice, fillings, toppings, and a small bowl or cup of water nearby.
8. Spread a thin layer of rice, leaving a 1-inch border at the top. You may need to dip your fingers into the water periodically to stop the rice from sticking.
9. Arrange tofu, avocado, cucumber, and jalapeño slices along the edge closest to you (the edge without the border).

recipe and ingredients continue

recipe continued from previous page

Spicy "crab stick"

1 block extra-firm tofu, pressed, drained, and patted dry.
½ cup vegan mayonnaise
2 tablespoons sriracha
1 tablespoon soy sauce (can sub tamari or coconut aminos)
2 teaspoons sesame oil

"Tuna"

5 Roma tomatoes
3 tablespoons soy sauce
½ tablespoon rice vinegar
1 sheet nori

Spicy "tuna" sauce

2 tablespoons vegan mayonnaise
1 teaspoon sesame oil
1 teaspoon sriracha
1 teaspoon soy sauce
Pinch of salt

Accompaniments (optional)

Jalapeños, sliced
Pickled ginger
Soy sauce
Wasabi

10. Lift the mat to roll, tucking as you go, forming a tight roll. When you get to the top of the roll that is not covered in rice, wet your fingers slightly and dab the water onto the nori sheet border and continue to roll until sealed. Set the sushi roll aside, seam side down.
11. Repeat with the remaining nori sheets and ingredients. Keep your sushi rolls in a cool place or refrigerator, covered, until ready to serve.
12. Using a very sharp knife, slice into 1-inch pieces, or about 8 pieces per roll.
13. Arrange your sushi on a platter and top with spicy "crab stick" or "tuna" and a drizzle of "eel" sauce. Serve alongside jalapeños, pickled ginger, soy sauce, and wasabi.

Eel sauce

1. In a small saucepan on medium-high heat, stir together the soy sauce, maple syrup, vinegar, and cornstarch.
2. Bring sauce to a boil, stirring frequently. Reduce heat to maintain a simmer and cook, still stirring, until sauce thickens slightly.
3. Remove from heat and let cool. Store, covered, in the refrigerator until ready to use.

Spicy "crab stick"

1. Shred the tofu block into a medium-sized bowl using the largest holes of a box or flat grater.
2. In a separate bowl, whisk together the mayonnaise, sriracha, soy sauce, and sesame oil.
3. Gently fold the tofu into the sauce. Some of the tofu will break apart; that's ok, it will still taste, and look, amazing.
4. Keep covered in the refrigerator until ready to use.

recipe continues

Note

This can be done without a sushi mat; the mat just makes it so much easier. If you don't have one, you can use parchment paper, plastic wrap, or just your hands.

Party tip

Make the eel sauce up to 5 days before your party and store it in an airtight container in the refrigerator.
Make the crabstick up to 4 days before your party and store it in an airtight container in the refrigerator.
Make the tomato tuna up to 2 days before your party and store it in an airtight container in the refrigerator.
While you can assemble your sushi rolls the day before your party and store them in the refrigerator, covered, it is best to make them the same day.

"Tuna"

1. First, start by blanching the tomatoes. Fill a medium pot with water and boil on high heat.
2. While you are waiting for the water to boil, score the tomatoes. If you are unfamiliar with this technique, it's quite simple. Get a sharp knife, like a paring knife. Make a shallow cut in the shape of an "X" at the base of the tomato. Make sure not to cut too deep into the tomato; you just want to cut the skin.
3. Get a medium or large bowl and fill it with cold water and ice. Set this on the counter near the stove.
4. Once the water is boiling, place the tomatoes in the pot. Boil them, stirring every 10 seconds or so to make sure they cook evenly, for about 30 to 60 seconds, or until you see the skin start to peel off.
5. Using a slotted spoon, remove the tomatoes and place them directly into the ice bath. Allow tomatoes to cool in ice water for 1 to 2 minutes.
6. Remove tomatoes from the water and peel off the skin.
7. Slice the tomatoes in half, then in half again (you now have 4 slices for each tomato). Scoop out and discard the seeds.
8. Combine the soy sauce and rice vinegar in a bowl. Add the tomatoes in with the marinade and gently stir to get them evenly coated with the sauce.
9. Tear the nori sheet into 4 or 6 big pieces and place them on top of the marinated tomatoes.
10. Cover the container and refrigerate for at least 3 hours or until ready to use.
11. After the tomatoes have marinated, remove them from the marinade and let them sit on a paper towel-lined plate to soak up the excess liquid. Roughly chop the tomatoes. Tomato tuna is ready to be used in sushi; if you would like it to be spicy, continue to the next step.
12. If you want to make the tomato tuna spicy, whisk together the spicy "tuna" sauce ingredients: mayonnaise, sesame oil, sriracha, soy sauce, and salt. Gently stir in the tomatoes.
13. Keep covered in the refrigerator until ready to use.

CAESAR SALAD CUPS

MAKES 12 SALAD CUPS

These are perfect for any type of party! They look fancy, taste delicious, and are super easy!

Dressing

½ cup unsalted cashews, soaked in just-boiled water for 10 minutes and drained
⅓ cup water, plus more if needed
1 ½ tablespoons lemon juice
1 tablespoon nutritional yeast
½ tablespoon capers, drained
½ tablespoon Dijon mustard
½ tablespoon vegan Worcestershire sauce
1 garlic clove, peeled
¼ teaspoon black pepper
¼ teaspoon salt

Salad cups

12 vegan wonton wrappers
2 ½ cups romaine lettuce, chopped
1 cup vegan "chicken" tenders, cooked according to package and diced
⅓ cup vegan croutons, roughly crushed or chopped
2 tablespoons vegan parmesan cheese*, grated (optional)

1. Preheat oven to 350°F and spray a muffin tin (standard size) with cooking spray.
2. To make the dressing, add all the dressing ingredients to a high-speed blender and blend until smooth and creamy, about 3 minutes. If the dressing is too thick, add more water, 1 tablespoon at a time, until you get the desired consistency. Keep covered in the refrigerator until ready to use.
3. Gently fit a wonton wrapper into each hole of the tin to form little cups and spray the wontons lightly with more cooking oil.
4. Bake for 8 to 10 minutes, until crispy and golden. Remove from the oven and set aside.
5. In a mixing bowl, combine the lettuce and the "chicken". Add ½ of the dressing. Toss gently to evenly combine. Add more dressing until the salad is perfectly coated as you like.
6. Divide the salad between the wonton cups. Top with croutons and vegan parmesan cheese. Serve immediately.

Party tip

Make your wontons the day before, let them cool completely, and store them in an airtight container at room temperature.
The dressing can be made up to 5 days in advance and stored in the fridge.

WONTONS IN SPICY CHILI SAUCE

SERVES 8 TO 10

Juicy dumplings filled with tender vegan beef and topped with a spicy chili sauce. Sophisticated yet nostalgic and soul-filling. These wontons are perfect for any occasion.

Dumplings

12- to 14-ounce package vegan beef crumbles, thawed if stated to in the package directions
2 green onions, chopped (white and light green parts)
2 tablespoons soy sauce
1 tablespoon cornstarch
1 tablespoon sesame oil
½ teaspoon black pepper
½ teaspoon garlic powder
½ teaspoon onion powder
½ teaspoon salt
½ teaspoon white pepper
1 package vegan wonton wrappers (will need about 40 to 50)

Garnish (optional)

Green onion, chopped

1. Cook vegan ground beef crumbles according to the package directions.
2. Remove from heat and add scallions, soy sauce, cornstarch, sesame oil, black pepper, garlic powder, onion powder, salt, and white pepper. Stir until evenly combined, then allow it to cool.
3. Once the filling has cooled, assemble your wonton station. You will need the filling, the wrappers, a damp towel or paper towel, a small bowl of water, a teaspoon, and a plate(s) to place the formed dumplings on.
4. Place a heaping teaspoon of the filling in the center of a wrapper. Place the damp towel on the remaining wrappers to prevent them from drying out.
5. Dip your finger in the water and lightly trace the edges of the wrapper, then fold it in half, bringing one corner to the opposite corner and making a triangle. Gently press out the air.
6. Bring the 2 side corners around to meet each other, wet 1 of the ends, and pinch them together to seal them.
7. Repeat with the remaining wrappers until all of the filling has been used.
8. Bring a large pot of water to boil. Carefully place wontons in water and cook until they float, about 3 to 5 minutes. Remove dumplings with a slotted spoon and transfer to a serving dish.
9. Drizzle the chili sauce over dumplings and garnish with green onions.

recipe and ingredients continue

recipe continued from previous page

Sauce

3 tablespoons chili oil
3 tablespoons soy sauce
3 cloves garlic, finely minced
2 tablespoons of water
1 tablespoon rice vinegar
2 teaspoons sesame oil
2 teaspoons sugar
1 teaspoon toasted sesame seeds
½ teaspoon chili flakes
½ teaspoon five-spice powder

Sauce

1. In a small pot, combine the chili sauce ingredients. Cook on low heat for about 5 to 10 minutes until the sugar has dissolved, stirring occasionally.
2. Remove from heat and drizzle on top of dumplings when ready to serve.

Party tip

You can assemble your wontons up to 3 months ahead of your party and freeze them prior to boiling. Lay them on a tray lined with parchment paper and freeze them for about 2 hours until firm. Once firm, transfer them to a freezer bag or container. Boil from frozen for about 5 to 8 minutes until dumplings float.

FALAFEL WITH TZATZIKI SAUCE

MAKES ABOUT 20

Crispy, tender falafel packed with chickpeas, herbs, and a jalapeño kick. Served with a creamy tzatziki sauce bursting with garlic, fresh herbs, and refreshing cucumber.

Falafel

1 cup dried chickpeas, soaked overnight *
1 cup yellow onion, roughly chopped
½ cup fresh parsley, roughly chopped
1 medium jalapeño, deseeded and roughly chopped
3 cloves garlic
1 teaspoon cumin
1 teaspoon ground coriander
1 teaspoon salt
½ teaspoon freshly ground black pepper
¼ teaspoon cayenne pepper
3 tablespoons all-purpose flour
½ teaspoon baking soda
Vegetable or canola oil for deep frying

Tzatziki dipping sauce

1 medium English cucumber
1 cup plain vegan yogurt
2 tablespoons fresh dill, finely chopped
2 cloves garlic, minced or pressed
1 tablespoon extra-virgin olive oil
1 tablespoon fresh parsley, finely chopped
2 teaspoons lemon juice
½ teaspoons sea salt

1. Drain and rinse chickpeas that were soaking overnight.
2. Add the chickpeas, onion, parsley, jalapeño, garlic, cumin, coriander, salt, pepper, and cayenne pepper to a food processor. Process until blended but not pureed. The mixture should look like coarse sand.
3. Add the flour and the baking soda and pulse 2 to 3 more times just to mix evenly.
4. Transfer mixture to a bowl, cover, and refrigerate for 1 to 2 hours or overnight if making ahead.
5. After the mixture is done chilling, use your hands or a spoon to shape the falafel using 1 ½ to 2 tablespoons of mixture each. If you are having trouble getting the falafel to stay together, add 1 to 2 more tablespoons of flour to the mix. If you are deep-frying the falafel, *which is how I think they taste best*, then form them into balls. They should be about 1 ½ to 2 inches in diameter. For baking, it is best to form the falafel into patties so you can flip them easier. They should be about 1 ½ to 2 inches in diameter and ½ inch thick.

recipe continues

recipe continued from previous page

Notes

* Soak your dried chickpeas overnight or for at least 12 hours. Make sure you cover them with 2 to 3 inches of cold water because they will triple in size. You might be asking, why the heck can't I just use canned chickpeas? You can, but the flavor is superior with dried chickpeas, and with canned, you can run into binding issues. It's another step, but it's worth it.

** Deep-frying: Exercise caution when deep-frying. These falafels are delicious AF, but nothing tastes good enough to warrant an oil burn. Make sure to use a deep pot, never leave the pot unattended, don't overfill or overcrowd the pot, and make sure to add the falafel gently to the oil so they don't cause splashing. Use a slotted spoon or tongs to add, flip, and remove falafel.

Party tip

Make your falafel batter and tzatziki sauce the day before and store them separately in an airtight container in the refrigerator.

6. Deep frying method: Once you have all the balls formed, heat about 3 inches of oil in a deep pot on medium heat to 350°F. Use a deep-fry thermometer to make sure the temperature is correct. If you don't have one, gently drop a pinch of the mixture into the oil; if it sizzles immediately, it is ready.
Cook the falafel in the oil, about 4 to 6 balls at a time, for about 3 minutes per side until they are golden brown. ****See safety note below.**
Remove with a slotted spoon and place falafel on a paper towel-lined plate.
Baking method: Preheat your oven to 425°F and grease a baking sheet with cooking spray or oil.
Transfer the falafel to the oiled baking sheet and, using cooking spray or a brush, lightly coat the top side of the patties with oil.
Bake for 15 minutes. Carefully flip patties over and continue to bake another 10 to 15 minutes until golden on both sides.
7. Transfer falafel to serving platter and serve with tzatziki dipping sauce.

Tzatziki dipping sauce

1. Grate the cucumber into a medium bowl and set aside.
2. In a separate bowl, whisk together the yogurt, dill, garlic, olive oil, parsley, lemon juice, and salt and set aside.
3. Wrap the grated cucumber in a kitchen towel or a paper towel and squeeze over the sink or the bowl to release the extra water. Try to get as much of the water out as possible.
4. Stir the grated cucumber into the dressing and serve alongside falafel as a dipping sauce.

CRABBY CAKES

MAKES ABOUT 16 CAKES

Luxurious, rich, and savory, these crabby cakes look and taste like their crustacean counterparts. Elegant enough for your holiday parties and easy enough to make for a last-minute get-together.

1 14-ounce can whole hearts of palm, drained
1 15.5-ounce can of chickpeas, drained and rinsed
1 14-ounce can whole artichoke hearts, drained and patted dry
1 red bell pepper, diced
3 green onions, diced
1 cup saltine crackers, crushed into crumbs (can sub panko breadcrumbs)
3 tablespoons chickpea flour
1 cup vegan mayonnaise
1 tablespoon Dijon mustard
1 tablespoon lemon juice
1 ½ tablespoons Old Bay Seasoning
½ teaspoon garlic powder
Vegetable oil for frying (optional)

Garnish (optional)
Fresh parsley, chopped
Lemon wedges

1. If you are baking these crabby cakes, preheat the oven to 400° F, line a baking sheet with parchment paper, spray the parchment paper with cooking spray, and set it aside.
2. Cut each heart of palm into 3 pieces, then shred or thinly slice each piece to mimic the look of crab. Set aside.
3. Add chickpeas and artichoke hearts to a food processor and pulse until chopped, with chunks remaining, about 5 to 8 times. Transfer to a large bowl and add the bell pepper, green onions, saltine crumbs, and chickpea flour, and gently stir to combine everything.
4. In a small bowl, whisk together the mayonnaise, mustard, lemon juice, Old Bay Seasoning, and garlic powder. Pour sauce into the chickpea and artichoke bowl and gently stir until everything is coated.
5. Gently fold in the hearts of palm until evenly distributed.
6. Scoop about ⅓ cup of the mixture into your hand and form a patty. If you are baking these patties, place them on the prepared baking sheet; otherwise, place them on a plate. Continue until you have used all of the chickpea mixture.
7. If you are baking crabby cakes, bake for 30 minutes, carefully flipping them over halfway. To pan-fry pour a shallow layer of oil in a frying pan and heat over medium heat for 2 to 3 minutes. While waiting for oil to heat, line 2 or 3 plates with paper towels.
8. Place 4 to 5 patties in the pan and fry for 3 to 4 minutes per side until golden brown and crispy. Transfer fried patties to the paper towels to absorb excess oil. Continue with remaining patties, adding oil if needed. Serve with fresh parsley, lemon wedges, and tartar sauce.

recipe and ingredients continue

recipe continued from previous page

Tartar sauce

1 cup dill pickles, finely chopped
1 cup vegan mayonnaise
2 tablespoons fresh dill, finely chopped (can sub fresh parsley)
1 teaspoon lemon juice
½ teaspoon Dijon mustard
½ teaspoon vegan Worcestershire sauce
¼ teaspoon black pepper
¼ teaspoon salt (optional)

Tartar sauce

1. Combine the pickles, mayonnaise, fresh dill, lemon juice, Dijon mustard, Worcestershire sauce, and black pepper in a mixing bowl and stir until evenly combined. Give it a taste and add salt if needed. *Dill pickles are quite salty, so they likely won't need any additional salt, but who am I to tell you how salty you should like your food?!*
2. Let the sauce chill in the refrigerator for at least 30 minutes before serving.

Party tip

Form the crabby cakes the night before but do not cook them. Keep them covered in the refrigerator. Bake or pan-fry just before your event and keep warm in the oven at 200°F.

You can make tartar sauce 5 days before your party and store it in an airtight container in the fridge.

BAKED TOFU SATAY WITH PEANUT DIPPING SAUCE

MAKES 12 SKEWERS

Tender tofu marinated in a flavorful blend of coconut milk, soy sauce, and Thai curry. Paired with a rich peanut sauce.

2 blocks super-firm tofu, drained and pressed (can sub extra-firm tofu)
½ cup coconut milk
2 tablespoons soy sauce (can sub tamari or coconut aminos)
1 tablespoon extra-virgin olive oil
1 teaspoon red Thai curry paste
½ teaspoon garlic powder
½ teaspoon salt
¼ teaspoon black pepper
¼ teaspoon ginger powder
12 skewers

Dipping sauce

½ cup creamy peanut butter
⅓ cup coconut milk
¼ cup water
2 tablespoons red Thai curry paste
1 tablespoon soy sauce (can sub tamari or coconut aminos)
1 tablespoon lime juice
1 teaspoon salt
½ teaspoon sesame oil

Garnish (optional)

¼ cup fresh cilantro, chopped
Handful of peanuts, slightly crushed

1. Slice each block of tofu into 6 long pieces, making 12 total.
2. Add all marinade ingredients to a mixing bowl and whisk until evenly combined.
3. Add tofu to a shallow dish and cover with the marinade. Chill the tofu in the fridge for at least 30 minutes, preferably overnight.
4. Preheat oven to 425°F and line a baking sheet with parchment paper.
5. Place the tofu on parchment paper and brush some of the marinade on top. Bake for 15 minutes. Turn the tofu over, brush again with some extra marinade, and continue baking for another 15 minutes.
6. While tofu is baking, make dipping sauce. Add all sauce ingredients to a medium mixing bowl and whisk to combine evenly. If the sauce is too thick, add a little more water, 1 tablespoon at a time.
7. Thread tofu pieces onto skewers lengthwise for a fun presentation (this is optional) and top with cilantro and crushed peanuts. Serve with dipping sauce.

Party tip

These taste better when marinated overnight, so make the tofu up to 3 days before your party. The dipping sauce can be made up to 5 days before your party. Both should be stored, separately, in airtight containers in the refrigerator.

SPICY ORANGE BBQ COCKTAIL MEATBALLS

MAKES ABOUT 30 COCKTAIL MEATBALLS OR 15 LARGE MEATBALLS

Tender seitan meatballs smothered in a sweet, smoky sauce with a jalapeño kick.

3 tablespoons olive oil, divided
1 cup yellow onion, roughly chopped
2 cloves garlic, minced
½ cup extra-firm tofu (slightly more than ¼ block)
½ cup vegetable broth
2 tablespoons nutritional yeast
2 tablespoons soy sauce (can sub tamari or coconut aminos)
1 tablespoon vegan Worcestershire sauce
2 teaspoons steak seasoning
1 teaspoon dried oregano
½ cup panko breadcrumbs
1 cup vital wheat gluten

Sauce

1 cup orange jam
1 cup barbecue sauce
1 jalapeño, deseeded and finely diced (love the heat? Make it 2!)
1 tablespoon soy sauce (can sub tamari or coconut aminos)
½ teaspoon salt

1. Heat 1 tablespoon of olive oil in a pan on medium heat.
2. Add onions and cook, stirring frequently, until tender, about 5 to 7 minutes.
3. Add garlic and cook, stirring continuously, for another 30 to 60 seconds. Remove from heat.
4. In a food processor bowl, add the onions and garlic, tofu, broth, nutritional yeast, soy sauce, Worcestershire sauce, steak seasoning, and oregano. Process on low or pulse until you reach a paste-like texture.
5. Add breadcrumbs and pulse again until mixed evenly. Transfer your mixture to a mixing bowl.
6. Add the wheat gluten and stir until the dough forms and there are no dry patches of flour remaining. You will probably have to put down the spoon and use your hands for this.
7. Shape the dough into your meatballs. For cocktail meatballs I like to go with ¾ to 1 inch; they will expand in the steaming process.
8. Set up your steamer by adding several inches of water to a pot and bringing it to a boil. Place the steamer basket on or in the pot, above the water level (make sure that the boiling water will not touch the basket). Line the basket with parchment paper (cut small holes in your parchment paper to allow steam to circulate if you are not using pre-perforated parchment rounds).

recipe continues

recipe continued from previous page

9. You will probably have to steam the meatballs in batches. Add meatballs to the steamer basket, cover, and steam for 12 minutes. Carefully turn meatballs over and steam for another 12 minutes.
10. You can store them in the refrigerator until you are ready to serve. Once ready, heat 2 tablespoons of olive oil in a pan on medium-high heat. Add the meatballs and cook until golden brown, turning the meatballs every 1 to 2 minutes. Now they are ready to be added to the sauce and served!

Sauce

1. Add sauce ingredients to a saucepan on medium heat. Cook, stirring occasionally, until sauce is heated, for about 10 minutes. Add meatballs to the sauce. Transfer to a serving dish and serve with a spoon or toothpicks.

Note

Steaming can be overwhelming at first, but once you get the hang of it, it's quite easy. I suggest getting a bamboo steamer if you are going to make it a habit to steam seitan. You can buy trays that stack, and they absorb excess moisture that could potentially make your food soggy. If you are unfamiliar with the steaming process and want to give it a try, whether with a bamboo basket or not, there are lots of videos online to guide you through the technique and demonstrate different basket methods. Happy steaming!

Party tip

Make the meatballs up to 4 days in advance of your party (but do not pan-fry) and store in an airtight container in the refrigerator.
The sauce can also be made in advance, up to 1 week, and stored in an airtight container.
On the day of serving, brown the meatballs in the pan, heat the sauce in a small saucepan on medium, combine, and serve!

HOLIDAY STUFFED MUSHROOMS

MAKES ABOUT 24 MUSHROOMS

Juicy, savory mushrooms stuffed with the delicious, nostalgic taste of the holiday season. Green bean casserole has long been a favorite at our Thanksgiving table. This stuffing is made with a decadent cashew cream sauce, mushrooms, onions, green beans, and yummy spices.

½ cup raw cashews
16 ounces cremini mushrooms
3 tablespoons extra-virgin olive oil, divided
⅓ cup yellow onion, diced
1 garlic clove, minced
1 tablespoon soy sauce (can sub tamari or coconut aminos)
2 teaspoons dry white wine or white cooking wine (can sub vegetable broth)
¼ teaspoon black pepper
⅛ teaspoon ground nutmeg
½ cup canned French-style green beans, drained and chopped (can sub regular-cut green beans)
¼ cup + 1 tablespoon crispy fried onions, crushed or chopped, divided
½ cup water

Party tip

These delicious appetizers can be made a day in advance by preparing the mushrooms, without the crispy onion garnish, covering them tightly, and storing them in the refrigerator. When you are ready to bake them, allow them to sit on the counter for 20 to 30 minutes, then sprinkle with the crispy onion garnish, and bake.

1. Place cashews in a heatproof bowl and cover with just-boiled water. Set aside for 30 minutes.
2. Preheat oven to 350°F. Lightly grease a wire rack and place it on a baking sheet with sides and set aside.
3. Remove the stems from the mushroom caps and set aside. Place caps in a bowl and drizzle with 2 tablespoons of oil. Use your hands or a spoon to toss the caps until all are evenly coated. Place caps on the wire rack and set aside. Dice the mushroom stems.
4. Heat 1 tablespoon of oil in a pan on medium heat. Once hot, add the onions and mushroom stems and sauté until the onions are tender and translucent, about 5 to 7 minutes.
5. Add garlic and cook 1 more minute, stirring frequently.
6. Stir in soy sauce, wine, pepper, and nutmeg, and cook for another 2 minutes.
7. Remove from heat and stir in green beans and ¼ cup crispy fried onions.
8. Drain cashews and add to a high-speed blender along with the water. Blend until smooth.
9. Add the cashew cream to the green bean mixture and stir until evenly combined.
10. Fill the mushroom caps with the green bean mixture.
11. Top with the remaining 1 tablespoon of crushed crispy onions.
12. Bake for 20 minutes.

JALAPEÑO PIEROGI

MAKES ABOUT 35 MINI OR 15 LARGE

Soft, tender dough filled with rich and creamy potatoes, spicy jalapeños, and vegan cheddar cheese.

Filling

2 large russet potatoes, peeled and chopped
4 tablespoons vegan butter, softened, divided
½ medium yellow onion, diced (save the rest to pan-fry with the pierogi, optional)
1 ½ cup jalapeños (about 4 or 5), seeded and diced
⅓ cup non-dairy milk, warmed
½ teaspoon black pepper
½ teaspoon salt
1 cup vegan shredded cheddar cheese

Dough

3 cups flour, plus little more for dusting
1 teaspoon salt
1 cup warm water
2 tablespoons extra-virgin olive oil

Serving

2 tablespoons vegan butter or extra-virgin olive oil
½ yellow onion, sliced (optional)
Vegan sour cream (optional)

Filling

1. Add potatoes to a pot and cover with water. Heat over high heat and bring to a boil. Turn heat down to maintain a low boil and cook until potatoes are fork-tender, about 15 to 20 minutes total. Drain potatoes when done and set aside.
2. Heat 1 tablespoon of vegan butter in a pan over medium heat. Add the diced onions and sauté, stirring occasionally, for about 5 to 8 minutes or until they begin to turn translucent.
3. Add the jalapeños to the pan and continue to sauté for another 5 to 8 minutes until the onions and peppers are tender and starting to brown. Remove from heat and set aside.
4. Add the drained potatoes to a large mixing bowl or back in the original pot. Using a hand or stand mixer, or a potato masher, break up the potatoes on low speed for about 30 seconds. Alternatively, if you have a potato ricer, press the potatoes through the ricer into the bowl or pot.
5. Add the remaining 3 tablespoons of butter, milk, pepper, and salt and continue to mix just until the potatoes are smooth and creamy. Do not overmix; potatoes can become gummy.
6. Gently stir in the onions, peppers, and shredded cheese.
7. Cover and chill in the refrigerator until ready to use, up to 3 days.

Dumplings

1. To make the dough, start by adding the flour and salt to a mixing bowl and mix.
2. Stir in the water and the oil and mix with a wooden spoon until a dough ball has formed.
3. Transfer dough onto a clean surface dusted with a little bit of flour and knead with hands for about 5 minutes, until smooth and soft. Form into a dough ball.

recipe continues

recipe continued from previous page

4. Place the dough ball in a bowl and cover and let rest for 15 to 30 minutes.
5. When you are ready to make the pierogi, split the dough ball into 2 or 3 smaller pieces.
6. Place one of the dough pieces on a lightly floured surface and roll it out to about ⅛ inch thick. Cut your desired size pierogi out. *I use a 2 ½-inch cookie cutter when I make my mini pierogi and a 3 ½ to 4-inch cookie cutter (or pint glass) when I make my regular-size pierogi.*
7. Continue to cut out your circles and roll out the dough until you have used all the dough.
8. Spoon the filling into each circle, about 2 teaspoons in a mini and 1 ½ tablespoons for the regular. The first circle will be the test of exactly how much you need for each pierogi.
9. Fold the circle in half over the filling and pinch around the edge to seal the dumpling. You may have to do this twice to make sure it's sealed. If you are having trouble getting the dough to seal, dip your fingers in a little bit of water and try again.
10. Continue until you have filled all the pierogi.
11. Pierogi can be frozen at this point (see note below) until you are ready to serve.
12. If you are ready to put the finishing touches on them, bring a pot of water to boil and go to the next step. If you are refrigerating, arrange them on a flat surface; make sure that they are not touching. Refrigerate covered. See notes below for freezing.
13. Add the pierogi to the boiling water; you can do this in multiple batches if need be. Gently stir the dumplings to make sure they are not sticking to the bottom of the pot or to each other. Boil for 3 to 5 minutes, or 6 to 8 minutes if they are frozen, until the pierogi begin to float.
14. Remove pierogi with a slotted spoon and set aside.
15. Melt butter or olive oil in a pan over medium heat. If you want fried onions with the pierogi, add them to the pan first and pan-fry for about 5 minutes, stirring occasionally to keep from burning.
16. Add pierogi and pan-fry for about 2 to 4 minutes on each side, until you've reached the desired crispiness.
17. Transfer to your serving platters with some vegan sour cream.

Party tip

Pierogi might just be my favorite food in the world to make; however, they do take some time. Fortunately, these can be in advance of your party. I suggest making these in a 3-part system:

Day 1: Make the filling.

Day 2: Stuff and freeze the pierogi.

Day 3 (weeks or months later): Boil and pan-fry the pierogi.

These can be frozen for up to 3 months. Arrange uncooked and preboiled pierogi on a baking sheet lined with parchment paper; make sure they are not touching. Freeze for 2 to 3 hours, until they are frozen solid, then transfer them to freezer bags or a freezer-friendly container.

FINGER FOODS

NEXT-LEVEL BRUSCHETTA

MAKES ABOUT 20 TOASTS

This recipe takes the classic dish to the next level by adding marinated artichoke hearts and hearts of palm.

- 1 cup cherry tomatoes, quartered
- ½ cup artichoke hearts marinated in oil, drained and chopped
- ½ cup hearts of palm, chopped
- 10 fresh basil leaves, thinly sliced
- 1 ½ tablespoons + ¼ cup extra virgin olive oil
- 1 teaspoon balsamic vinegar
- ¼ teaspoon pepper
- ¼ teaspoon salt
- 1 baguette loaf, sliced into ¼- to ½ -inch-thick slices
- 1 garlic clove, peeled and halved
- Balsamic glaze to drizzle (you will need about ⅓ cup)

1. In a medium bowl, add the tomatoes, artichokes, hearts of palm, basil, 1 ½ tablespoons of olive oil, balsamic vinegar, salt, and pepper. Gently stir to combine. Set aside to marinate for at least 20 minutes.
2. Preheat oven to 400°F and line a baking sheet with tin foil.
3. Brush both sides of each of the baguette slices with the remaining ¼ cup of olive oil and arrange on a baking sheet.
4. Bake for 8 to 10 minutes, until the slices are golden brown and crisp.
5. Rub each top side of the bread with the garlic clove, cut side down. You want to do this while the bread is still hot, but not so hot that it burns your fingers!
6. Arrange the bread on your serving dish, garlic side up.
7. Spoon the tomato mixture over each of the toasts.
8. Drizzle the balsamic glaze over top and serve immediately.

Party tip

Make the tomato-artichoke topping in the morning and store it in the refrigerator. Make the garlic bread toasts 30 minutes before guests arrive and arrange them on your serving platter, covered with tin foil. As soon as you are ready to serve, add the topping and drizzle.

BASIL RICOTTA CROSTINI

MAKES ABOUT 12 TO 16 CROSTINI

Crunchy bread topped with creamy fresh basil ricotta and garlic tomatoes. This appetizer is so easy to make yet looks and tastes gourmet. Perfect for a holiday party.

Crostini

1 French baguette, thinly sliced about ½ inch thick (can sub bread of choice)
2 to 3 tablespoons extra-virgin olive oil

Basil ricotta

14- to 16-ounce block extra-firm tofu, drained and pressed
½ cup fresh basil
½ cup nutritional yeast
¼ cup non-dairy milk
1 tablespoon extra-virgin olive oil
1 tablespoon lemon juice
1 teaspoon garlic powder
1 teaspoon salt
½ teaspoon black pepper

Tomato topping

1 cup cherry or grape tomatoes, sliced in half
1 tablespoon extra-virgin olive oil
1 garlic clove, minced or pressed
1 teaspoon balsamic vinegar
¼ teaspoon black pepper
¼ teaspoon salt

1. Preheat oven to 400°F and line a baking sheet with parchment paper. Set aside.
2. To make the tofu ricotta, add tofu, basil, nutritional yeast, milk, 1 tablespoon olive oil, lemon juice, garlic powder, salt, and pepper to a food processor. Pulse until ingredients are evenly combined and texture is smooth. Set aside "ricotta".
1. Brush both sides of the baguette with olive oil and place on a baking sheet. Bake for about 9 to 12 minutes, until the bread is crisp and lightly golden on top.
2. To make the tomato topping, heat 1 tablespoon olive oil on medium heat in a small or medium pan.
3. Add garlic and sauté for about 30 seconds, stirring constantly, making sure the garlic does not burn.
4. Add tomatoes and sauté for another minute.
5. Add the balsamic vinegar, salt, and pepper and cook another 3 to 4 minutes, until the tomatoes are tender. Remove from heat.
6. Transfer the ricotta mixture to a piping bag and pipe, in a back-and-forth motion, the ricotta on each crostino.*
7. Spoon the tomatoes on top of each crostino and serve.

Note

*If you do not have a piping bag, you can get the same effect by cutting the corner off a freezer or sandwich bag. If you do not care to have the piped look on the crostini, you can also spread the ricotta on the crostini with a knife, it all tastes the same!

Party tip

Make the basil ricotta and the tomato the day before and store separately, in airtight containers, in the refrigerator. Warm the tomatoes before topping the crostini in the microwave for 30 seconds to 1 minute.

LOADED SHEET PAN NACHOS

SERVES 6 TO 8

Nachos just might be the perfect food. So many incredible flavors in 1 bite. Easy to customize, easy to share. These nachos should be the centerpiece of your table. Pairs perfectly with margaritas!

1 ½ cups water
1 teaspoon or cube vegan beef bouillon (can sub vegetable bouillon)
1 cup TVP
1 tablespoon soy sauce (can sub tamari or coconut aminos)
½ tablespoon tomato paste
1 teaspoon cumin
1 teaspoon garlic powder
1 teaspoon smoked paprika
1 teaspoon vegan Worcestershire (can sub vegan steak sauce)
½ teaspoon black pepper
1 tablespoon extra-virgin olive oil
½ cup yellow onion, diced
2 cloves garlic, minced or pressed
10- to 14.5-ounce package tortilla chips
15-ounce can black beans, drained and rinsed
2 cups vegan shredded cheddar cheese
1 to 2 fresh jalapeños, sliced (deseeded if you want them less spicy)
4-ounce can sliced black olives, drained
½ cup cherry tomatoes, halved or quartered
⅓ cup red onion, diced

1. Preheat oven to 400°F and line a baking sheet with parchment paper or aluminum foil; set aside.
2. Bring 1 ½ cups of water to a boil and dissolve 1 teaspoon of vegan beef bouillon or cube (or vegetable bouillon).
3. Add TVP to a small bowl and pour 1 cup of the just-boiled water on top. Set aside to rehydrate for at least 10 minutes.
4. In a separate small or medium bowl, add the remaining ½ cup of the broth, soy sauce, tomato paste, cumin, garlic powder, smoked paprika, Worcestershire sauce, and pepper. Whisk to fully combine and set aside.
5. Heat olive oil in a pan over medium heat. Add onions and cook until translucent, for about 5 minutes, stirring occasionally.
6. Add in the garlic and sauté another minute, stirring frequently.
7. Add in the TVP and the marinade. Stir together and reduce heat to medium-low. Continue to cook, stirring occasionally, until the liquid has been absorbed, approximately another 3 to 5 minutes.
8. Layer the tortilla chips on the baking sheet.
9. Assemble the nachos by spooning the TVP crumbles evenly on top of the chips. Next the black beans, followed by the cheese. Add the jalapeños and the olives.
10. Bake for 5 to 10 minutes, until the cheese has melted.
11. Remove from oven and top with tomatoes, onions, and cilantro.
12. Drizzle sauces on top or serve alongside nachos as dips.

recipe and ingredients continue

recipe continued from previous page

Garnish (optional)
Fresh cilantro, chopped

Avocado lime crema
2 ripe medium avocados, pitted and peeled
3 tablespoons fresh lime juice (about 2 medium limes or 1 large lime)
½ cup vegan sour cream
2 cloves garlic, minced
¼ cup fresh cilantro
1 teaspoon salt
1 teaspoon black pepper
¼ cup dairy-free milk (optional if too thick)

Salsa sour cream sauce
1 cup vegan sour cream
½ cup of your favorite salsa, smooth or chunky

Avocado lime crema
1. Add all of the avocado lime crema ingredients, except the milk, into a food processor or blender and blend on high until creamy and smooth. Make sure to scrape down the sides to include all the yummy bits of cilantro. If sauce is too thick, add unsweetened dairy-free milk, in 1 tablespoon increments, and continue to blend until you get the desired consistency.
2. Transfer to a bowl to serve alongside your nachos, or top the nachos with sauce using a piping bag or squeeze bottle.

Salsa sour cream
1. Blend together the sour cream and the salsa. You can use a spoon and just stir together to combine if you are using a smooth salsa. *I prefer to blend either way.* If it comes out too thin (if you are using a very watery salsa), add more sour cream in 1 to 2 tablespoon increments and continue to blend or mix until you get the desired consistency.
2. Transfer to a bowl to serve alongside the nachos, or drizzle on top using a squeeze bottle or a piping bag.

Party tip
Make the TVP crumbles and avocado and salsa sauces up to 3 days in advance of your party and store in an airtight container in the refrigerator.

SEITAN CHICKEN FINGERS

MAKES ABOUT 12 TO 16 LARGE PIECES

These crowd-pleasing vegan chicken fingers are seasoned to perfection and baked until crispy. They go great with all the yummy vegan sauces in this book!

Seitan chicken

1 tablespoon vegetable oil
1 cup yellow onion, roughly chopped
1 cup cannellini beans, drained and rinsed
½ cup water
2 tablespoons nutritional yeast
2 tablespoons soy sauce (can sub tamari or coconut aminos)
1 teaspoon garlic powder
1 teaspoon onion powder
1 teaspoon vegan chicken bouillon or 1 cube (or vegetable bouillon)
12 ounces silken tofu
2 cups vital wheat gluten

Seitan chicken

1. Heat oil in a pan or skillet over medium-high heat. Add onions and sauté until the onions turn translucent and begin to brown, about 5 minutes.
2. Stir in the cannellini beans, water, soy sauce, nutritional yeast, garlic powder, onion powder, and bouillon. Sauté for another 2 minutes to let the flavors combine.
3. Add the onion and bean mixture to a food processor along with the silken tofu and process until smooth.
4. Add the vital wheat gluten and pulse 2 to 4 times until just combined. Do not overmix because it will affect the texture.
5. Lay a sheet of parchment paper or tin foil on the counter and dump the seitan on top. Form into a square-like piece that is about 1 inch thick.
6. Cut the seitan into 4 to 6 equal pieces. Wrap each piece individually in tin foil; make sure not to wrap them tight. They will expand a little, so you want to allow some room for that.
7. Now we are going to steam them. Put a steamer basket in a large pot and add an inch or two of water, making sure the water does not touch the bottom of the steamer basket.
8. Bring the water to a simmer. Place the seitan pieces in the basket, cover, and steam for 15 minutes. After 15 minutes, carefully flip the seitan pieces over, using tongs. Be careful of the steam! Steam for another 15 minutes and remove from heat.

recipe and ingredients continue

recipe continued from previous page

Coating

1 cup non-dairy unsweetened milk
1 tablespoon lemon juice
1 cup vegan breadcrumbs
2 tablespoons nutritional yeast
1 teaspoon Adobo all-purpose seasoning (can sub 1 teaspoon salt)
1 teaspoon black pepper
1 teaspoon garlic powder
1 teaspoon onion powder
1 teaspoon smoked paprika
1 cup all-purpose flour

Party tip

Make seitan chicken up to 4 days before your party and store it in the refrigerator, covered. On the morning of your party, slice and dredge your seitan fingers, then place them back in the refrigerator until ready to bake. If stacking seitan, place a sheet of parchment paper in between.

9. Remove the seitan from the aluminum foil and allow them to cool. From here you can store them in the fridge until ready to serve. When you are ready to serve these "chicken" strips, you are going to want to slice each of the 4 to 6 large pieces into smaller strips. How small you make your chicken slices is up to you. You can make them bite-sized or long, thin strips.

Chicken fingers

1. Preheat the oven to 425°F and line a baking sheet with parchment paper. Set aside.
2. Mix milk and lemon juice in a bowl and let sit for 1 to 2 minutes. The mixture will begin to thicken and curdle; this is now your vegan buttermilk.
3. In a separate bowl, combine the breadcrumbs, nutritional yeast, Adobo seasoning, garlic powder, onion powder, and smoked paprika.
4. In a 3rd bowl, add the flour.
5. Take a seitan strip and dip it into the flour. Shake off excess flour.
6. Dip it into the vegan buttermilk and shake off excess liquid.
7. Repeat the last 2 steps: dip the seitan back into the flour, shaking off excess, and back into the buttermilk, once again shaking off excess.
8. Roll the seitan in the crumb mixture, covering the entire strip, and place on a baking sheet.
9. Repeat this process for each of the seitan fingers.
10. Spray both sides of the seitan chicken with cooking oil or use a basting brush to lightly brush on oil.
11. Bake for 15 minutes, flip the seitan over, and bake for another 10 to 15 minutes, until the seitan is crispy and golden brown. Serve with your favorite vegan dipping sauces (check out chapter "SAUCE ON THE SIDE" on pg. 143).

PHILLY EGGLESS ROLLS

MAKES 12 TO 16 ROLLS

Savory plant-based meat, gooey cheese, and fried onions and peppers. Just a couple swaps to make this super popular dish vegan.

- 16 ounces vegan beef crumbles, thawed if package instructions require it
- 3 to 4 tablespoons olive oil, divided
- 1 medium or large green bell pepper, diced
- 1 medium yellow onion, diced
- 1 medium jalapeño, seeded and diced
- ½ teaspoon salt
- 1 tablespoon Worcestershire sauce
- ½ teaspoon black pepper
- ½ teaspoon garlic powder
- ½ teaspoon onion powder
- ½ teaspoon smoked paprika
- ⅔ cup vegan cheese, shredded or chopped slices (provolone, cheddar, or mozzarella)
- 1 package vegan egg roll wrappers
- 4 to 6 cups vegetable oil for frying (can sub canola or peanut oil)*

1. Cook the vegan crumbles according to package directions and set aside.
2. Add 2 tablespoons of oil to a pan or skillet and heat over medium heat. Add the bell pepper, onion, jalapeño, and salt and cook, stirring occasionally, until tender, about 5 to 7 minutes.
3. Add the crumbles to the pan with the peppers and onions and stir in the Worcestershire sauce, black pepper, garlic powder, onion powder, and smoked paprika.
4. Stir in the shredded cheese and cook for another 2 to 3 minutes, until the cheese begins to melt. Remove from heat.
5. Set up your assembly station with the egg roll wrappers, the filling, a plate or tray to place the finished egg rolls, and a small bowl or cup with some water to dip your fingers.
6. Place a wrapper on a clean surface, the points facing up and down (like a diamond), and spoon about 3 tablespoons of filling on the center of the wrapper.
7. Use a pastry brush or your fingers to brush a small amount of water on the top edge of the wrapper.
8. Pull the bottom corner of the wrapper up over the filling, then fold each of the sides in, and continue to roll up the wrapper, keeping it tight, until sealed.
9. Set aside, seam side down, and continue with additional wrappers until you've used all the filling.

recipe continues

recipe continued from previous page

10. In a frying skillet, wok, or pot, add 2 to 3 inches of oil and heat over medium heat for about 5 minutes, until 350°F is reached.
11. Carefully add egg rolls into the oil. Cook in batches and make sure not to crowd them, about 3 or 4 at a time. Cook until golden brown and crispy, about 3 to 5 minutes, turning them occasionally to ensure even browning.
12. Carefully remove with a slotted spoon and place on a paper towel-lined plate to drain excess grease. Repeat until all egg rolls are fried.
13. Serve egg rolls whole or sliced in half diagonally with your choice of dipping sauces.

Note

*You would rather bake egg rolls instead of frying? While they do taste better fried, this is your party. To bake the egg rolls, preheat the oven to 400°F and line a baking sheet with parchment paper. Brush or spray each roll with oil and place, seam side down, on the baking sheet. Bake for 8 to 10 minutes, flip, and bake another 8 to 10 minutes, until golden and crispy. Enjoy!

Party tip

Assemble the egg rolls the day before your party, but do not cook them. Store them in the refrigerator, seam side down, covered. Make sure to let the filling cool completely before rolling the egg rolls if you intend to make these ahead to prevent the wrappers from getting soggy from the steam.

CRABLESS MELTS

MAKES 8 MELTS

Crab melts were a holiday season staple in my childhood home. My mom would make them while we decorated our Christmas tree. In this recipe, shredded tofu takes the place of crabmeat. These melts are deliciously crispy, meaty, and cheesy. Add them to your holiday party menu, summer bash, or birthday celebration. They will definitely be a hit!

4 vegan English muffins
8 ounces super-firm tofu, drained and pressed (can sub extra-firm)
1 cup vegan shredded cheddar cheese*
3 tablespoons vegan mayo
1 ½ tablespoons vegan butter, softened
1 teaspoon Old Bay seasoning
½ teaspoon garlic powder
¼ teaspoon black pepper
¼ teaspoon celery salt
¼ teaspoon onion powder

Garnish (optional)
Fresh parsley, chopped

Party Tip
Make the tofu topping the night before or morning of and store it in the refrigerator in an airtight container.

1. Preheat oven to 350°F and line a baking sheet with tin foil.
2. Split the English muffins and arrange on a baking sheet; set aside.
3. Shred tofu using the large grate size of a cheese grater.
4. In a medium mixing bowl, add the shredded cheese, mayo, butter, Old Bay, garlic powder, pepper, celery salt, and onion powder. Mix until combined.
5. Carefully fold in the shredded tofu. **
6. Spread the mixture equally on the 8 muffin halves and bake for 20 minutes.
7. Switch the stove setting to broil and broil for 2 additional minutes, or until the cheese looks bubbly and the edges are starting to crisp.
8. Transfer to your serving dish and garnish with fresh parsley.

Notes
*I like to use 2 different brands of cheddar cheese, ½ cup each. You can use your favorite shredded vegan cheddar for the full 1 cup, but I think using multiple brands gives a little more depth to the cheese flavor.
**The tofu will break apart easily, so be careful when combining with the other ingredients. The shape and size of the tofu are merely to mimic crab, so even if the majority of it crumbles, do not panic—it will still taste great!

MINI GRILLED CHEESE WITH TOMATO SOUP DIP

MAKES ABOUT 15 SANDWICHES

Grilled cheese and tomato soup is one of the most perfect pairings around. This grilled cheese is cheesy, crispy, and seasoned to perfection. Accompanied by a creamy tomato soup flavored with garlic and fresh basil. Perfect for a birthday party, game day, holiday party, or snow day gathering!

Grilled cheese

½ cup vegan butter, softened
1 tablespoon vegan mayo
1 teaspoon garlic powder
½ teaspoon black pepper
½ teaspoon dried basil
½ teaspoon dried oregano
½ teaspoon dried parsley
1 long French baguette, thinly sliced (about ⅜ inch thick)
2 packages of vegan cheese slices (15 to 20 slices)*

Tomato soup

3 tablespoons vegan butter
1 medium yellow onion, diced
2 cloves garlic, minced or pressed
28-ounce can whole tomatoes
2 teaspoons dried oregano
1 teaspoon kosher salt
½ teaspoon black pepper
½ teaspoon crushed red pepper flakes
½ cup fresh basil, chopped
⅓ cup coconut cream
¼ cup nutritional yeast

Grilled cheese

1. Preheat the oven to 400°F and line a baking sheet with aluminum foil.
2. In a small bowl, mix the butter, mayo, garlic powder, black pepper, basil, oregano, and parsley.
3. Spread the butter mixture on 1 side of ½ of the bread slices, placing them on the baking sheet butter side down.
4. Fold a cheese slice in half and place both halves on top of the bread. If you are using 2 different flavors of cheese, use ½ of each. Repeat until all the bread slices on the baking sheet are topped with cheese.
5. Butter 1 side of the remaining bread slices and top the sandwiches on the baking sheet with the butter side up.
6. Bake sandwiches for 10 minutes. Flip the sandwiches over and bake for another 5 minutes.
7. Transfer to a serving platter and serve by themselves or alongside tomato soup dipping sauce.

Tomato soup

1. Melt the butter in a medium or large pot over medium-high heat. Add the onions and sauté for 4 to 7 minutes until lightly browned.
2. Add the garlic and sauté for another minute.

recipe continues

recipe continued from previous page

3. Add the whole tomatoes, including the liquid, oregano, salt, pepper, and red pepper flakes, and bring to a boil. Then drop the heat down to low or medium-low and simmer for 15 minutes.
4. Stir in the fresh basil, coconut cream, and nutritional yeast and let simmer for another 2 minutes. Remove from heat.
5. Next up is blending the soup. You can use an immersion blender or a regular (countertop) blender. Just make sure if you are using the latter, you let it cool down for at least 15 minutes first.
6. Transfer to your serving dish for dipping, or pour into shot glasses or mini cups, and serve alongside your mini grilled cheese sandwiches.

Note

* I suggest getting 2 different flavored vegan cheese slices, if you have that available in stores near you. I like to use both cheddar and provolone. If you are using 2 different flavors, you will use ½ a slice of each cheese on each sandwich.

Party tip

Make your tomato soup up to 3 days before your party and store it in an airtight container in the refrigerator. Reheat in a saucepan on medium heat, stirring frequently, or in the microwave in 30-second intervals, stirring each time.

QUESADILLAS FOR A CROWD

MAKES ABOUT 16 SLICES

Crisp and cheesy quesadillas filled with meaty tofu, onions, peppers, and black beans. These are so good they might make your carnivore friends go vegan! Seriously, they're the best.

Tofu "chicken"

1 block extra-firm tofu, drained and pressed
¼ cup nutritional yeast
1 teaspoon chili powder
¼ teaspoon garlic powder
¼ teaspoon ground cumin
¼ teaspoon onion powder
¼ teaspoon salt
¼ teaspoon smoked paprika
Pinch of cayenne pepper (optional, if you like spicy)

Tofu "chicken"

1. Preheat oven to 350°F and line a baking sheet with parchment paper.
2. Cut the tofu into ⅓- to ½-inch cubes and set aside.
3. In a large bowl mix together all the tofu seasonings.
4. Add the tofu to the bowl. Using your hands or spoons, toss the tofu until evenly coated. I like to do this in a sealable container and then shake it.
5. Transfer the tofu to the baking sheet with the parchment paper and bake for 35 minutes.
6. Remove from heat and set aside. Keep the oven at 350°F.

Quesadillas

1. If you are skipping the tofu or made that in advance, preheat the oven to 350°F.
2. Heat the oil in a large skillet over medium heat.
3. Add the onions, peppers, black beans, and green chiles. Cook, stirring frequently, for about 5 to 7 minutes, until vegetables are tender.
4. Add the chili powder, pepper, cumin, garlic powder, onion powder, salt, and smoked paprika. Stir it all up and cook for another minute, then remove from heat.

recipe and ingredients continue

recipe continued from previous page

Quesadillas

2 tablespoons extra-virgin olive oil
1 yellow onion, chopped
1 red pepper, chopped
15-ounce can black beans, drained and rinsed
5-ounce can mild green chiles (or hot if you want to add some kick)
1 teaspoon chili powder
½ teaspoon black pepper
½ teaspoon cumin
½ teaspoon garlic powder
½ teaspoon onion powder
½ teaspoon salt
½ teaspoon smoked paprika
10 medium (10-inch) flour tortillas
16 ounces shredded vegan cheese (Mexican blend, cheddar, or half cheddar and half mozzarella blend)

5. Time to assemble! Spray a 9x13 sheet pan with cooking spray. Place 2 flour tortillas in the center so they cover most of the pan, like a figure 8, but have them slightly overlap.
6. Now place 6 more tortillas around the edges. 1 on each of the short sides and 2 on the long sides. They should all be half in the pan, overlapping with the 2 in the center, and half hanging off the pan (we're going to fold them over eventually).
7. Sprinkle ½ of the shredded cheese evenly on the tortillas across the whole sheet pan, followed by the bean filling, the tofu, and then the remaining cheese.
8. Take the last 2 tortillas and place them on top of the quesadilla filling, just like you did to start (the figure 8), again slightly overlapping.
9. Fold all the tortillas over on top to close the quesadilla. *I like to fold the 2 on the ends first, then fold the 4 on the sides, but it really doesn't matter the order.*
10. Spray the top of the quesadilla with cooking spray and cover with a piece of tin foil—you do not need to wrap it, just lay it on top. Place another baking sheet on top of the tin foil to hold the quesadilla in place. Bake for 20 minutes.
11. Remove the pan on top, along with the tin foil. Place back in the oven and bake for another 10 minutes at 400°F. The quesadilla is done when the tortillas are crispy.
12. Remove from heat and let cool for about 10 minutes before slicing.

Party tip

Make the tofu "chicken" and the vegetables up to 3 days before your party and store separately, in airtight containers, in the refrigerator.

CHEESY GARLIC BREAD

MAKES ABOUT 10 SLICES

This one has all the heavy hitters: crispy bread, garlic butter, and melted cheese. The perfect comfort food.

1 loaf French or Italian bread
½ cup vegan butter, softened
3 garlic cloves, finely minced
½ tsp dried basil
½ tsp dried oregano
½ tsp garlic powder
2 cups vegan shredded cheddar cheese

Garnish (optional)
¼ cup fresh parsley, chopped

Serving (optional)
1 cup marinara, warmed, for dipping

1. Preheat the oven to 400°F and line a baking sheet with tin foil.
2. Slice the bread lengthwise and place on the baking sheet, crust down, sliced side up.
3. Stir together the butter, garlic, basil, oregano, and garlic powder in a mixing bowl.
4. Spread half of the seasoned butter evenly over each of the loaf halves.
5. Top each half with 1 cup of vegan shredded cheese, spread out evenly.
6. Bake for 14 to 16 minutes, or until desired crispiness. Remove from oven, slice into pieces, garnish with fresh parsley, and serve alongside marinara sauce for dipping.

Party tip
Make the butter in advance and store it, covered, in the refrigerator. Let it soften on the counter for about 30 minutes before spreading on the bread.

SHEET PAN PIZZA

SERVES 6 TO 8

What's a party without pizza? This cheesy pizza delivers with a light and crispy crust and a savory and spicy sauce. The best pizzas are the ones we eat with friends!

Pizza

Extra-virgin olive oil, for greasing
1 pizza dough (recipe below) or store-bought vegan pizza dough at room temperature
1 to 1 ½ cups pizza sauce (recipe below) or store-bought
2 cups vegan shredded mozzarella or cheddar cheese
¼ cup grated vegan parmesan cheese
6 to 10 fresh basil leaves
Red pepper flakes (optional)

Dough

2 cups all-purpose flour OR bread flour, divided
1 packet instant yeast (2 ¼ teaspoon)
1 teaspoon sugar
1 teaspoon salt
½ teaspoon garlic powder
2 tablespoons olive oil, plus additional for greasing
¾ cup warm or lukewarm water, NOT HOT, or it will kill your yeast

Pizza

1. Preheat the oven to 450°F and grease a sheet pan with olive oil.
2. Use your fingers to stretch the pizza dough to fit the pan as best as possible. It's ok if it doesn't completely cover the pan.
3. Top the dough with the pizza sauce, spreading it evenly but leaving a ½-inch border for the crust.
4. Next, top with the shredded cheese.
5. Bake for 20 to 25 minutes, or until the crust is golden brown and crispy and the cheese is bubbling and slightly browned.
6. Remove from oven and let sit for 5 to 10 minutes. Top with grated vegan parmesan, fresh basil leaves, and red pepper flakes.

Cut into the desired number of slices and enjoy!

Dough

1. Add 1 cup of flour, the instant yeast, sugar, salt, and garlic powder to a large mixing bowl. Stir to evenly combine with a wooden spoon.
2. Stir in 2 tablespoons olive oil and the warm water.
3. Gradually add another cup of flour, stirring, until the dough forms an elastic but still slightly sticky ball. Lightly dust your hands with some flour and finish forming the dough into a ball.
4. Get another clean mixing bowl and drizzle some olive oil around the sides. Use a pastry brush or a paper towel to coat the entire bowl with the oil.
5. Place your dough ball into the oil-coated bowl and gently roll the dough around so that the dough becomes coated with oil.

recipe and ingredients continue

recipe continued from previous page

Pizza Sauce

1 tablespoons olive oil
½ small yellow onion (about ½ cup), chopped
1 teaspoon dried oregano
½ teaspoon dried basil
½ teaspoon red pepper flakes (don't like spicy—don't add it! Or maybe just ¼ teaspoon)
2 cloves garlic, pressed or minced
14.5-ounce can peeled whole tomatoes
½ teaspoon salt
½ teaspoon sugar

Party tip

Make the dough up to 2 days before your party and store it in the refrigerator, wrapped tightly in plastic wrap. When you are ready to make your pizza, let the dough sit out for 1 to 2 hours on the counter to bring it to room temperature.

Make your sauce up to 5 days before your party and store it in the refrigerator in an airtight container.

6. Tightly cover the bowl with plastic wrap, lay a towel on top, and set aside in a warm, dry place for 1 hour, or until the dough doubles in size.
7. Gently punch down with your fist in the center of the pizza dough to deflate the dough and let the built-up gas out.
8. Knead it for a minute or 2, and now it is ready to be used for pizza! At this point you can continue to the next step, or, if you are making the dough in advance, wrap it tightly with plastic wrap and store it in the refrigerator for up to 2 days. When you are ready to use it, let the dough sit out for 1 to 2 hours to bring it to room temperature before shaping it.

Sauce

1. Add the olive oil to a small saucepan on medium-high heat.
2. Once heated, add the onions, oregano, basil, and red pepper flakes. Cook for about 5 to 7 minutes, stirring occasionally, until onions become translucent and tender.
3. Reduce heat to medium and add the garlic. Cook for another 30 seconds to a minute, stirring so the garlic does not burn.
4. Add the tomatoes, salt, and sugar, and give it a good stir to combine.
5. Bring the sauce to a gentle boil, then lower the heat to maintain a simmer. Let simmer for about 20 minutes, stirring occasionally. Remove from heat.
6. Use an immersion blender to blend the sauce until it is smooth, or a little chunky if that is the way you like your sauce. If you don't have an immersion blender, use a countertop blender, but make sure you let the sauce cool down first for at least 15 minutes.

BAKED GARDEN FRIES

SERVES 6 TO 8

Potatoes, green beans, and carrots are seasoned and baked until crispy. They pair perfectly with all the yummy vegan sauces in this book! Happy dipping!

2 russet potatoes, cut into ¼-inch-thick strips (skin on or off)
12 ounces green beans, ends trimmed off
12 ounces carrot sticks
2 tablespoons olive oil
1 ½ tablespoons cornstarch
1 teaspoon garlic powder
1 teaspoon onion powder
1 teaspoon salt
½ teaspoon black pepper
½ teaspoon smoked paprika

Garnish (optional)
Fresh parsley, chopped

1. Preheat oven to 425°F and line a baking sheet, or sheets, with parchment paper. You can cook all 3 fry types on the same baking sheet or bake the green beans and carrots on 1 sheet and the potatoes on a separate sheet.
2. In a large bowl, toss the potatoes, green beans, and carrot slices with the oil, cornstarch, and seasonings until evenly coated.
3. Lay the fries on the baking sheet in a single layer and bake for 20 to 30 minutes, flipping halfway.
4. Garnish with fresh parsley (optional) and serve immediately with your favorite dipping sauces. (check out chapter "SAUCE ON THE SIDE" on pg. 143)

Party tip
Make the fries up to 2 hours prior to your party and keep them at room temperature uncovered. Reheat in the oven for 5 minutes just before serving, and top with parsley garnish.

HEARTY MAINS

THE BEST CHILI

SERVES 6 TO 8

The gang's all here. The game is just about to start. The beer is on ice. And your chili bar is a hit! Whatever the score, you've won today!

2 tablespoons olive oil
1 yellow onion, diced
2 jalapeño peppers, seeded and diced
1 poblano pepper, seeded and diced
3 garlic cloves, pressed or minced
2 tablespoons tomato paste
28-ounce can fire-roasted diced tomatoes
2 ½ cups vegetable broth
15.5-ounce can red kidney beans, drained and rinsed
15.5-ounce can cannellini beans, drained and rinsed
15.5-ounce can pinto beans, drained and rinsed
1 cup TVP (textured vegetable protein)
2 tablespoons chili powder
1 tablespoon cocoa powder
2 teaspoons or 2 cubes vegan beef bouillon (optional)
1 teaspoon cinnamon
1 teaspoon cumin
1 teaspoon smoked paprika
1 teaspoon salt
1 teaspoon black pepper

1. In a large pot over medium heat, heat oil. Add onion and peppers and cook, stirring occasionally, until tender and translucent, about 6 to 8 minutes.
2. Add garlic and tomato paste and cook for another minute, stirring constantly.
3. Stir in the remaining ingredients: tomatoes, broth, beans, TVP, chili powder, cocoa powder, bouillon, cinnamon, cumin, smoked paprika, salt, and pepper.
4. Increase heat to medium-high and bring to a boil, then reduce heat to medium-low or low and maintain a simmer. Simmer for 40 minutes.
5. Serve with a variety of toppings or over fries or nachos.

Note

Set up your chili bar with a variety of customizable toppings such as chopped fresh cilantro, sliced jalapeños, diced red onion, tortilla chips, vegan shredded cheddar cheese, and vegan sour cream.

Party tip

This chili tastes even better on day 2, so make this ahead of time and store it in the refrigerator, covered. Reheat on the stove over medium heat for 5 to 10 minutes, stirring frequently. Then transfer to a serving dish or slow cooker.

BURGERS ON THE GRILL

MAKES ABOUT 6 BURGERS

It's burger time! Filled with meaty flavor and texture, these burgers are perfect for your cookout or tailgate.

1 cup TVP
1 cup just-boiled water
1 teaspoon vegan beef bouillon (can sub vegetable bouillon)
2 tablespoons extra virgin olive oil
1 cup yellow onion, roughly chopped
12 ounces cremini mushrooms, chopped
15.5-ounce can red kidney beans, drained and rinsed
2 tablespoon soy sauce (can sub tamari or coconut aminos)
1 tablespoon Worcestershire sauce
2 teaspoons steak seasoning
1 teaspoon garlic powder
½ cup sun-dried tomatoes in oil
⅓ cup panko breadcrumbs
⅓ cup wheat gluten

1. Place TVP in a small bowl and cover with just-boiled water. Mix in 1 teaspoon of bouillon and set aside for 15 minutes until the water has been absorbed.
2. Heat oil in a pan on medium-high heat. Add onions and cook, stirring occasionally, for about 2 to 3 minutes, until they begin to soften.
3. Add mushrooms and cook for another 5 to 7 minutes until mushrooms are beginning to brown.
4. Stir in the kidney beans, soy sauce, Worcestershire sauce, steak seasoning, and garlic powder and let cook for another minute.
5. Transfer the onion mixture to a food processor and add in the sun-dried tomatoes. Process on low or pulse until finely minced and almost paste-like, stopping occasionally to scrape down the sides of the bowl. It's ok to have some chunks for texture.
6. Add in the breadcrumbs and give it a quick pulse or 2 to evenly combine the breadcrumbs.
7. Transfer to a mixing bowl and add vital wheat gluten. Mix the vital wheat gluten with a spoon, or your hands, until thoroughly combined.
8. Form into burger patties.
9. Now it's time to steam them! Add several inches of water to a pot and bring to a boil. Add a steamer basket and make sure the basket is not touching the water. Add the burgers to the basket, cover, and steam for 30 minutes, flipping halfway (see note on additional steaming instructions).

recipe continues

recipe continued from previous page

10. Store burgers in the fridge in an airtight container until ready to use. When you are ready to serve them, pan-fry or grill them on medium-high heat for 3 to 6 minutes on each side, until you get a nice brown or char and they are heated through.

Note

Steaming seitan can be overwhelming at first, but once you get the hang of it, you will be steaming seitan every week! You want to make sure the seitan does not get wet, so the basket should not touch the water, even as it is boiling. You can steam these burgers in a bamboo basket, but you will have to do it in batches, unless you have a stacking basket. I prefer to use a metal steaming basket inserted into the pot (you can even make a DIY steaming basket with tin foil and a plate; check out videos online). Wrap the burgers individually in tin foil, allowing a little space to expand, then stack them on top of each other in the steaming basket and cover. At the halfway point, I take them out and rearrange which ones were on the top and the bottom of the stack for even cooking. Be careful when removing the burgers from the steamer—steam is hot!!

Party tip

These burgers get even better the next day, so make them up to 4 days in advance of your party, store them in the refrigerator, then fire up the grill!

MEATBALLS AND RED SAUCE

MAKES ABOUT 30 SMALL 15 LARGE MEATBALLS

Tender, meaty seitan balls, spiced to perfection, and smothered in a savory red sauce. From tailgates to holiday parties, meatballs are always a hit.

Meatballs

3 tablespoons olive oil, divided
1 cup yellow onion, roughly chopped
2 cloves garlic, minced
½ cup extra-firm tofu (slightly more than ¼ block)
½ cup vegetable broth
2 tablespoons nutritional yeast
2 tablespoons soy sauce (can sub tamari or coconut aminos)
1 tablespoon vegan Worcestershire sauce
2 teaspoons vegan beef bouillon (can sub vegetable bouillon)
1 teaspoon dried basil
1 teaspoon dried oregano
1 teaspoon dried parsley
½ teaspoon black pepper
½ cup panko breadcrumbs
1 cup vital wheat gluten

Meatballs

1. Heat 1 tablespoon olive oil in a pan on medium heat
2. Add onions and cook, stirring frequently, until tender, about 5 to 7 minutes.
3. Add garlic and cook, stirring continuously, for another 30 to 60 seconds. Remove from heat.
4. In a food processor bowl, add the onions and garlic, tofu, broth, nutritional yeast, soy sauce, Worcestershire sauce, bouillon, basil, oregano, parsley, and pepper. Process on low or pulse until you reach a paste-like texture.
5. Add breadcrumbs and pulse again until mixed evenly. Transfer your mixture to a mixing bowl.
6. Add the wheat gluten and stir until the dough forms and there are no dry patches of flour remaining. You will probably have to put down the spoon and use your hands for this.
7. Shape the dough into your meatballs. For cocktail meatballs I like to go with ¾ to 1 inch; they will expand in the steaming process.
8. Set up your steamer by adding several inches of water to a pot and bringing it to a boil. Place the steamer basket on or in the pot, above the water level (make sure that the boiling water will not touch the basket). Line the basket with parchment paper (cut small holes in your parchment paper to allow steam to circulate if you are not using pre-perforated parchment rounds).

recipe and ingredients continue

recipe continued from previous page

Red sauce
2 tablespoons olive oil
1 cup yellow onion, diced
3 garlic cloves, finely minced or pressed
28 ounces crushed tomatoes (including juice)
1 ½ teaspoon dried oregano
1 teaspoon salt
½ teaspoon black pepper
¼ cup fresh basil (can sub 2 teaspoons dried basil)
¼ cup fresh parsley (can sub 2 teaspoons dried parsley)

Party tip
Make the meatballs (but do not pan-fry) and sauce up to 4 days in advance of your party and store them, separately, in airtight containers in the refrigerator.
On the day of serving, brown the meatballs in the pan, heat the sauce in a saucepan on medium, combine, and serve!

9. You will probably have to steam the meatballs in batches. Add meatballs to the steamer basket, cover, and steam for 12 minutes. Carefully turn meatballs over, and steam for another 12 minutes.
10. You can store them in the refrigerator until you are ready to serve. Once ready, heat 2 tablespoons of olive oil in a pan on medium-high heat. Add the meatballs and cook until golden brown, turning the meatballs every 1 to 2 minutes. Now they are ready to be added to the sauce and served over spaghetti or in hoagie rolls with vegan cheese, or by themselves.

Red sauce
1. Heat oil in a medium pot over medium heat. Add onions and cook, stirring occasionally, until tender and translucent, about 5 to 7 minutes.
2. Add garlic and cook for another minute, stirring constantly so garlic does not burn.
3. Add the tomatoes (with the juice), dried oregano, salt, and black pepper. If you are using dried basil and parsley instead of fresh, add that in now as well.
4. Cover and simmer on low for 20 to 30 minutes, stirring occasionally.
5. Stir in the fresh basil and parsley, cover, and simmer for an additional 5 to 10 minutes.
6. Use an immersion blender or countertop blender to blend the sauce until the desired consistency is reached (optional step).

Note
Steaming can be overwhelming at first, but once you get the hang of it, it's quite easy. I suggest getting a bamboo steamer if you are going to make it a habit to steam seitan. You can buy trays that stack, and they absorb excess moisture that could potentially make your food soggy. If you are unfamiliar with the steaming process and want to give it a try, whether with a bamboo basket or not, there are lots of videos online to guide you through the technique and demonstrate different basket methods. Happy steaming!

SEITAN CHICKEN AND STEAK FAJITAS

SERVES 6 TO 8

There's something extra fun about a build-your-own station. These fajitas have 2 types of meaty seitan proteins to go with the traditional vibrant, savory, and smoky fajita flavors.

Fajita seasoning (can sub 1 store-bought packet)
½ tablespoon chili powder
½ tablespoon ground cumin
1 teaspoon garlic powder
½ teaspoon onion powder
½ teaspoon paprika
½ teaspoon salt
¼ teaspoon black pepper
¼ teaspoon cayenne pepper (omit if you don't like hot spice)

Seitan chicken
2 tablespoons vegetable oil, divided
1 cup yellow onion, roughly chopped
1 cup cannellini beans, drained and rinsed
½ cup water
2 tablespoons soy sauce (can sub tamari or coconut aminos)
2 tablespoons nutritional yeast
½ tablespoon fajita seasoning
1 teaspoon vegan chicken bouillon or 1 cube (or vegetable bouillon)
12 ounces silken tofu
2 cups vital wheat gluten

Fajita seasoning
1. Mix the fajita seasoning ingredients together and store in a small jar or container until ready to use. Alternatively, you can use a store-bought packet of fajita seasoning.

Seitan chicken strips
1. Heat 1 tablespoon of oil in a pan or skillet over medium-high heat. Add onions and sauté until the onions turn translucent and begin to brown, about 5 minutes.
2. Stir in the cannellini beans, water, soy sauce, nutritional yeast, fajita seasoning, and bouillon. Sauté for another 2 minutes to let the flavors combine.
3. Add the onion and bean mixture to a food processor along with the silken tofu and process until smooth.
4. Add the vital wheat gluten and pulse 2 to 4 times until just combined. Do not overmix.
5. Lay a sheet of parchment paper or tin foil on the counter and dump the seitan on top. Form into a square-like piece that is about 1 inch thick.
6. Cut the seitan into 4 to 6 equal pieces. Wrap each piece individually in tin foil; make sure not to wrap them tight. They will expand a little, so you want to allow some room for that.

recipe and ingredients continue

recipe continued from previous page

Seitan steak
2 tablespoons vegetable oil, divided
1 cup yellow onion, chopped
1 cup canned lentils, rinsed and drained
½ cup water
2 tablespoons soy sauce (can sub tamari or coconut aminos)
2 tablespoons tomato paste
2 tablespoons nutritional yeast
1 tablespoon vegan Worcestershire sauce
1 teaspoon vegan beef bouillon, or 1 cube (can sub vegetable bouillon)
1 teaspoon smoked paprika
1 teaspoon garlic powder
1 teaspoon onion powder
½ teaspoon salt
½ teaspoon black pepper
1 ½ cups vital wheat gluten

Steak marinade
3 tablespoons water
2 tablespoons soy sauce (can sub tamari or coconut aminos)
2 tablespoons balsamic vinegar
2 tablespoons vegetable oil
1 tablespoon vegan Worcestershire sauce
½ tablespoon fajita seasoning
1 teaspoon vegan beef bouillon, or 1 cube (can sub vegetable bouillon)

Veggies
1 tablespoon vegetable oil
2 to 3 red, orange, or yellow bell peppers, sliced
1 white onion, sliced
½ tablespoon fajita seasoning

Fajitas
Flour tortillas

Seitan steak strips
1. Heat 1 tablespoon of oil in a pan or skillet over medium-high heat. Add onions and sauté until the onions turn translucent and begin to brown, about 5 minutes.
2. Stir in the lentils, water, soy sauce, tomato paste, nutritional yeast, Worcestershire sauce, vegan beef bouillon, smoked paprika, garlic powder, onion powder, salt, and pepper. Sauté for another 2 minutes to let the flavors combine.
3. Add the onion and lentil mixture to a food processor and process until smooth.
4. Add the vital wheat gluten and pulse 2 to 4 times until just combined. Do not overmix.
5. Lay a sheet of parchment paper or tin foil on the counter and dump the seitan dough on top. Form into a square-like piece that is about 1 inch thick.
6. Cut the seitan into 4 to 6 equal pieces. Wrap each piece individually in tin foil; make sure not to wrap them tight. They will expand a little, so you want to allow some room for that.
7. Now we are going to steam them. Put a steamer basket in a large pot and add an inch or two of water, making sure the water does not touch the bottom of the steamer basket.
8. Bring the water to a simmer. Place the seitan pieces in the basket, cover, and steam for 15 minutes. After 15 minutes, carefully flip the seitan pieces over, using tongs. Be careful of the steam! Steam for another 15 minutes and remove from heat.
9. Remove the seitan from the aluminum foil and allow them to cool. From here you can store them in the fridge until ready to serve. When you are ready to serve these "chicken" strips, you are going to want to slice each of the 4 to 6 large pieces into smaller strips. How small you make your slices is up to you. You can make them bite-sized or long, thin strips.
10. Heat 1 tablespoon of vegetable oil in a pan over medium-high heat. Add the seitan and pan-fry for 4 to 8 minutes, flipping the pieces as you go, until you reach the desired crispiness.

recipe continues

recipe continued from previous page

7. Now for the steaming, put a steamer basket in a large pot and add a few inches of water, making sure the water does not touch the bottom of the steamer basket.
8. Bring the water to a simmer. Place the seitan pieces in the basket, cover, and steam for 15 minutes. After 15 minutes, carefully flip the seitan pieces over, using tongs. Be careful of the steam. Steam for another 15 minutes.
9. Remove the seitan from the aluminum foil and place in a deep container with a lid. Make the marinade.
10. Whisk the marinade ingredients together in a small mixing bowl.
11. Pour marinade evenly over seitan pieces and let marinate in the refrigerator for at least 1 hour, preferably overnight.
12. When you are ready to serve these "steak" strips, you are going to want to slice each of the 4 to 6 large pieces into smaller strips. Just like the "chicken" seitan, how small you make your slices is up to you. You can make them bite-sized or long, thin strips, *which is what I prefer.*
13. Heat 1 tablespoon of vegetable oil in a pan over medium-high heat. Add the seitan and pan-fry for 4 to 8 minutes, flipping the pieces as you go, until you reach the desired crispiness.

Veggies

1. Heat vegetable oil in a pan over medium-high heat. Add vegetables and fajita seasoning and stir so the veggies are evenly seasoned.
2. Cook peppers and onions until tender and crisp, about 6 to 10 minutes. Serve alongside the seitan chicken and steak.

Party tip

This recipe takes some time, but it is worth it! Make seitan chicken and steak up to 4 days before your party and store them in the refrigerator, covered. Day of, you just need to slice and pan-fry!

Set up your fajita station with your protein and veggies, flour tortillas, and an assortment of toppings or add-ons such as avocado slices, lime wedges, pico de gallo, rice, salsa, vegan shredded cheese, or vegan sour cream.

TOFU AND BLACK BEAN ENCHILADAS

MAKES 8 WHOLE OR 16 HALVED

Hearty shredded tofu and black beans covered in a savory sauce and melted cheese. These enchiladas are so delicious, so comforting, and so filling—even the meat eaters will be going back for more.

Sauce

1 tablespoon olive oil
2 garlic cloves
2 ½ cups tomato sauce
½ cup vegan chicken broth (can sub vegetable broth)
2 tablespoons nutritional yeast
2 teaspoons chili powder
2 teaspoons cumin
1 teaspoon black pepper
1 teaspoon dried oregano
1 teaspoon onion powder
1 teaspoon salt

Enchiladas

1 14- to 16-ounce block super-firm tofu, drained and pressed (can sub extra-firm tofu)
1 tablespoon extra-virgin olive oil
1 medium yellow onion, diced
1 garlic clove, minced or pressed
15-ounce can black beans, drained and rinsed
Homemade enchilada sauce, divided (can sub 3 cups store-bought)
1 ½ cup vegan shredded cheddar cheese, divided
8 large flour tortillas

Sauce

1. Make the sauce first by heating 1 tablespoon of oil in a small or medium saucepan over medium heat.
2. Add garlic and sauté for about 30 seconds, stirring constantly, so the garlic does not burn.
3. Add in the remaining sauce ingredients, stir, and bring to a simmer.
4. Simmer for 3 minutes and remove from heat.

Enchiladas

1. Preheat the oven to 350°F.
2. Shred the tofu using the large holes of a box or cheese grater. Set aside.
3. Heat oil in a large pan on medium heat. Add onions and sauté, stirring occasionally, until onions become translucent, approximately 5 to 7 minutes.
4. Add garlic and cook an additional 30 seconds, stirring.
5. Add black beans and ½ cup of the homemade enchilada sauce and sauté for an additional 2 to 3 minutes, stirring occasionally.
6. Remove from heat and mix in 1 cup shredded cheese.
7. Carefully fold in the shredded tofu. *Some of the tofu will break, and that is ok. It will still taste amazing!*

recipe and ingredients continue

recipe continued from previous page

Garnish (optional)
Fresh cilantro, chopped
2 avocados, pitted, peeled, and sliced
Vegan sour cream

8. Pour 1 cup of the enchilada sauce into a 9x13 (or similar size) baking dish. Spread it out evenly across the bottom with a spoon or a spatula.
9. Take 1 tortilla and spoon ½ to ¾ cup of the shredded tofu and bean mixture down the center. Roll the tortilla up and place it in the baking dish, on top of the sauce, seam side down. Repeat for each of the tortillas.
10. Pour the remaining enchilada sauce evenly over the top of the enchiladas.
11. Top with the remaining ½ cup shredded cheese.
12. Bake, uncovered, for 20 to 25 minutes, until the cheese is melted. Serve whole or halved. Top with fresh cilantro (optional).

Party tip
Make the sauce and the tofu-bean filling the day before. Store them in the refrigerator separately, covered. That way all you have left to do is assemble and bake.

CAJUN STUFFED PEPPERS

MAKES 6 OR 12 STUFFED PEPPERS

Dirty rice is the inspiration for these peppers. While dirty rice is typically made with ground meat, this dish has 2 types of vegan protein, creating a complex flavor profile and an enhanced meaty texture.

Peppers

7 bell peppers, divided: 6 peppers whole and 1 pepper chopped (varying in color of green, yellow, orange, or red)
2 tablespoons extra-virgin olive oil
½ yellow onion, chopped
1 celery stalk, chopped
3 garlic cloves, finely minced or pressed
2 teaspoons dried parsley
2 teaspoons smoked paprika
2 teaspoons soy sauce
2 teaspoons vegan Worcestershire sauce
1 teaspoon dried oregano
1 teaspoon dried thyme
1 teaspoon garlic powder
1 teaspoon onion powder
½ teaspoon black pepper
½ teaspoon salt
2 cups cooked rice
1 ½ cup vegan shredded cheddar cheese, divided

1. Preheat the oven to 400°F and line a baking sheet with parchment paper.
2. The first step is to prep the peppers; cut and deseed the 6 whole peppers. You have 2 ways to cut the peppers; the first is by cutting the top off so that the pepper sits upright when stuffed. While I do think this looks best, if you are making these for a party at which the peppers are not the main course, I suggest the second way. The second way is to cut the peppers in half lengthwise (and remove the stem). This will make each pepper produce 2 stuffed peppers that lie on their side; 6 peppers become 12 servings. There is no wrong answer—it's up to you.
3. Place peppers with the cut side up on the baking sheet. Drizzle a little olive oil over each pepper. Rub the oil over each of the peppers, using a paper towel, a basting brush, or your hands, and place them back down cut side up.
4. Sprinkle a little salt over each of the peppers and bake for 20 minutes. Once 20 minutes have passed, remove peppers from the oven. Drain the excess water that has accumulated in the peppers and set them aside.
5. Replace the parchment paper on the baking sheet with a fresh sheet and set the oven to 350°F.
6. Make the tofu by chopping it into small pieces, about ½ inch cubes, and set aside.
7. In a medium bowl, whisk together the remaining tofu ingredients.

recipe and ingredients continue

recipe continued from previous page

Tofu

14-ounce block extra-firm tofu, drained and pressed
3 tablespoons nutritional yeast
2 tablespoons extra-virgin olive oil
2 tablespoons soy sauce
1 teaspoon garlic powder
1 teaspoon onion powder
1 teaspoon poultry seasoning

TVP

1 cup water
2 teaspoons soy sauce
2 teaspoons vegan beef bouillon (can sub vegetable bouillon)
2 teaspoons vegan Worcestershire sauce
1 teaspoon liquid smoke
1 cup TVP

Garnish (optional)

Fresh parsley, chopped

Note

This recipe involves prepping 2 types of protein: tofu and TVP. If you want to make this a bit easier, feel free to pick just one of these proteins. It will still taste great whichever one you go with, but the combination definitely takes it to the next level.

8. Add tofu to the bowl with seasoning paste and gently stir to coat.
9. Spread tofu on baking sheet and bake for 35 minutes. After 35 minutes, remove from oven and set aside. Keep the oven set to 350°F.
10. Now let's prep the TVP. Add water to a small saucepan. Stir in soy sauce, bouillon, Worcestershire sauce, and liquid smoke and bring to a boil.
11. Remove from heat and add the TVP to the pan, gently stirring to make sure all the TVP gets covered. Set aside for 10 minutes, until the liquid is absorbed.
12. Add 2 tablespoons olive oil to a large sauté pan. Heat over medium-high heat. Add chopped peppers, onions, and celery. Sauté for about 7 to 9 minutes, until veggies are tender.
13. Add garlic and sauté for another minute, stirring.
14. Stir in the parsley, smoked paprika, soy sauce, Worcestershire sauce, oregano, thyme, garlic powder, onion powder, pepper, and salt.
15. Add in the rehydrated TVP and sauté for another minute.
16. Next you want to combine the vegetables and TVP with the baked tofu, cooked rice, and cheese. If you have enough room in the sauté pan, great—one less dish to clean! If not, transfer the veggies to an extra-large mixing bowl and add the baked tofu, cooked rice, and 1 cup of the vegan shredded cheddar cheese. Stir to combine everything evenly.
17. Assemble the peppers. Place the peppers, cut-side up, in a baking dish. Fill each pepper with the rice mixture. Top each pepper with the remaining ½ cup vegan shredded cheddar cheese.
18. Cover with tin foil and bake for 20 minutes. Remove the tin foil and continue to bake another 10 to 15 minutes, until the cheese is melted. Top with some chopped fresh parsley (optional).

Party tip

Stuff the peppers, cover, and store them in the refrigerator the day before your party. Let the dish chill on the counter for about 30 minutes before baking.

EGGPLANT ROLLATINI

SERVES 6 TO 8

This vegan version of the classic Italian American dish has a creamy tofu cheese filling infused with fresh basil.

2 medium or large eggplants, sliced lengthwise (¼-inch thick slices)
2 to 4 teaspoons salt (to salt the eggplant), plus additional 1 teaspoon
3 to 4 tablespoons extra-virgin olive oil (for brushing eggplant), plus additional 1 tablespoon
1 block extra-firm tofu (14 to 16 ounces), drained and pressed
½ cup fresh basil
½ cup nutritional yeast
¼ cup non-dairy milk
1 tablespoon lemon juice
1 teaspoon dried oregano
1 teaspoon garlic powder
½ teaspoon black pepper
2 ½ cups marinara, divided
¾ cup vegan shredded mozzarella cheese

1. Preheat oven to 400°F and line a baking sheet with parchment paper.
2. Lightly salt both sides of the eggplant slices and let them sit for 10 to 15 minutes to sweat out the excess moisture. Pat them dry and wipe off salt.
3. Arrange eggplant slices on the baking sheet and brush both sides with olive oil. Bake for about 10 minutes, just until tender. Remove from oven and set aside to cool.
4. To make the tofu filling, add tofu, basil, nutritional yeast, milk, 1 tablespoon olive oil, lemon juice, oregano, garlic powder, 1 teaspoon salt, and pepper to a food processor. Pulse until ingredients are evenly combined and texture is smooth. Set aside.
5. Spread 1 cup of the marinara on the bottom of your baking dish.
6. Spoon 1 to 2 tablespoons of the tofu filling onto the wider end of each of the eggplant slices. Spread the filling across the bottom ⅔ of the slice.
7. Gently roll the eggplant slices and place them in the baking dish with the sauce, seam-side down.
8. Top the rollatini with the remaining marinara sauce and the shredded cheese.
9. Bake for 30 minutes, covered. Remove the cover and bake for an additional 10 minutes, until the cheese is melted and bubbly. Allow to cool for about 10 minutes before serving.

Party tip

Assemble the rollatini a day or 2 before your party and refrigerate it, unbaked and covered. Allow the dish to sit on the counter for about 30 minutes before baking.

SWEET AND SPICY VEGGIE PASTA

SERVES 6 TO 8

Inspired by lo mein, this pasta dish is packed with bold umami flavor and loaded with colorful produce.

Pasta

16-ounce package short pasta of choice
2 tablespoons vegetable oil
1 ½ cup shredded carrots
12 ounces cremini or button mushrooms, sliced
1 ½ cups sugar snap peas or snow peas
1 red pepper, thinly sliced
1 green bell pepper, thinly sliced
2 garlic cloves, minced or pressed

Sauce

1 cup vegetable broth (or water)
⅓ cup vegetable oil
4 tablespoons soy sauce (can sub tamari or coconut aminos)
2 tablespoons dark soy sauce*
2 tablespoons hoisin sauce
2 tablespoons potato starch (can sub corn starch)
2 teaspoons sesame oil
1 ½ teaspoons garlic powder
1 ½ teaspoons onion powder
1 teaspoon ground ginger
1 teaspoon sugar
½ to 1 teaspoon crushed red pepper flakes
½ teaspoon white pepper

Garnish (optional)

3 to 4 spring onions, finely chopped
2 teaspoons toasted sesame seeds

1. Cook pasta according to the package directions until al dente. Drain pasta and set aside.
2. While the pasta is cooking, make the sauce by combining all the ingredients for the sauce into a medium mixing bowl and whisking together.
3. Heat vegetable oil in a large pan over medium-high heat. Add the carrots to the pan and sauté for about 2 minutes, stirring frequently.
4. Add the mushrooms, snap peas, and peppers. Continue cooking until the vegetables are tender, approximately 3 to 5 more minutes.
5. Add the garlic and sauté for another 30 seconds, stirring frequently.
6. Add the sauce to the pan, reduce heat to medium-low, and bring to a simmer.
7. Add the pasta to the pan. Stir it all up so the pasta is coated and mixed with the vegetables. Simmer for 1 minute. Remove from heat.
8. Transfer to a serving dish and garnish with spring onions and toasted sesame seeds. Serve warm.

Note

*If you cannot find dark soy sauce, just use 6 tablespoons of regular soy sauce.

Party tip

Make the sauce and store it in an airtight container in the refrigerator up to 2 days before your party. Prep the carrots, snap peas, and peppers the day before and store them in the refrigerator in an airtight container.

CREAMY SPINACH PASTA BAKE

SERVES 6 TO 8

Creamy pasta with spinach and onions. Perfect for game days, holiday gatherings, potlucks, or any time you want something delicious, comforting, and filling.

1 cup unsalted cashews
16 ounces short pasta (like penne)
1 tablespoon extra-virgin olive oil
1 cup yellow onion, diced
2 garlic cloves, pressed or minced
¼ cup dry white wine
1 tablespoon soy sauce (can sub tamari or coconut aminos)
1 teaspoon black pepper
1 teaspoon crushed red chili pepper flakes (optional, if you like spicy)
1 teaspoon salt
3 cups fresh baby spinach, (optional: stems trimmed off)
1 cup water
1 cup vegan mozzarella shredded cheese, divided

Party tip

This dish can be assembled and refrigerated, prior to baking, the day before your party. Keep it covered while in the refrigerator and let it sit out for about 30 minutes before baking.

1. Place cashews in a heat-safe bowl, cover with just-boiled water, and set aside.
2. Cook pasta according to directions on box, drain, and set aside.
3. Preheat oven to 350°F and grease or spray a 9x13 baking dish (or similar size) and set aside.
4. Heat oil in a large pan over medium heat. Add onion and sauté until tender, about 5 to 7 minutes.
5. Add garlic and cook another minute, stirring frequently.
6. Stir in dry wine, soy sauce, black pepper, crushed red pepper, and salt and cook another 2 minutes, stirring occasionally.
7. Turn off heat and add spinach. Continue to toss the spinach in the pan until the spinach has just wilted, about 1 to 2 minutes.
8. Drain cashews and add to a high-speed blender or food processor. Add 1 cup water and blend until completely smooth.
9. Grab a large mixing bowl, unless everything can fit in the pan, and gently mix the cashew cream, pasta, onions, and spinach, and ½ cup of the shredded cheese until it is evenly combined.
10. Spread out evenly in the baking dish and top with the remaining ½ cup shredded cheese.
11. Bake for 20 to 25 minutes, uncovered, until the cheese on top has melted. Allow to cool for about 10 to 15 minutes before serving. Dig in!

PASTALAYA

SERVES 6 TO 8

This savory pasta features onions, peppers, and celery (aka the holy trinity) with bold Cajun spices. Mix in your favorite vegan sausage to turn a delicious side dish into a hearty main.

16-ounce short pasta (like penne or farfalle)
12 to 16 ounces vegan sausage links (optional), sliced into bite-sized pieces
3 tablespoons extra-virgin olive oil, divided (2 tablespoons if you are not using sausage)
1 medium yellow onion, diced
1 medium green bell pepper, diced
1 medium red bell pepper, diced
2 celery stalks, diced
4 Roma tomatoes, chopped
3 garlic cloves, minced
2 teaspoons smoked paprika
1 teaspoon dried basil
1 teaspoon garlic powder
1 teaspoon onion powder
1 teaspoon vegan chicken bouillon or vegetable bouillon (or 1 cube)
½ teaspoon black pepper
½ teaspoon salt
¼ teaspoon cayenne pepper (omit if you don't like spicy)
3 tablespoons vegan butter

1. Cook pasta according to the directions on the package. Drain and set aside.
2. If you are using vegan sausage, add 1 tablespoon of olive oil to the pan and heat over medium heat. Add the sausage links and cook until each side begins to crisp, about 4 to 6 minutes on each side depending on the brand. Remove from the heat and set aside.
3. In a sauté pan or medium pot, add 2 tablespoons of oil and heat over medium-high heat. Add the onions, peppers, and celery. Sauté, stirring frequently, until they begin to soften, for about 5 to 7 minutes.
4. Add the tomatoes, garlic, smoked paprika, basil, garlic powder, onion powder, bouillon, black pepper, and salt. Cook for a minute on medium-high heat, then reduce to medium heat and continue to cook, stirring occasionally, for another 5 minutes so all the flavors marry.
5. Turn off heat and add the vegan butter. Stir it around until it's completely melted and mixed within the veggies.
6. Add the pasta and the sausage (if you're using it) to the pan and gently mix everything together until it is evenly combined. Transfer to your serving dish and enjoy!

Party tip

You can make this dish up to 2 days ahead of your party and store it in an airtight container in the refrigerator. Reheat on the stove over medium heat. The pasta will have absorbed most of the liquid, so add a splash of water or broth.

BAKED MAC AND CHEESE

SERVES 8 TO 10

Rich, cheesy pasta topped with crispy, buttery, seasoned breadcrumbs. Deliciously gooey. Pairs well with football, holidays, and friends.

Mac and cheese

16 ounces large or jumbo elbow macaroni (or short your pasta of choice)
½ cup vegan butter
½ cup all-purpose flour
2 ½ cups unsweetened non-dairy milk
2 tablespoons nutritional yeast
1 ½ teaspoons salt
1 teaspoon black pepper
1 teaspoon garlic powder
1 ¼ cups vegan shredded cheddar cheese

Crispy topping

1 cup vegan panko breadcrumbs
1 tablespoon nutritional yeast
1 teaspoon smoked paprika
½ teaspoon black pepper
½ teaspoon salt
¼ cup vegan butter, melted

Party tip

Assemble the mac and cheese without the breadcrumb topping and store it in the refrigerator, covered. Let the dish sit out on the counter for about 30 minutes, then top with the crispy breadcrumbs and bake.

1. Preheat the oven to 400°F and lightly spray a 9x9 (or similar size) baking dish with nonstick spray or lightly grease with vegetable oil.
2. Cook the pasta until al dente according to the directions on the package. Drain pasta and set aside.
3. In a medium pot or large pot, melt ½ cup butter over medium heat. Add the flour and whisk to combine. Keep whisking constantly for about 1 minute; the flour will start to smell yummy and buttery.
4. Slowly add the milk, whisking continuously. Cook, while whisking frequently, for about 5 minutes, until the sauce begins to thicken. Add the nutritional yeast, salt, pepper, and garlic powder and whisk to combine.
5. Next, add the shredded cheese and continue to whisk until the shredded cheese melts.
6. Add the pasta to the cheese sauce pot, or the sauce to the pasta pot, whichever one fits them both. Gently stir around, making sure all of the pasta is coated.
7. Transfer the pasta to the baking dish. Make sure to scrape all the cheesy goodness from the sides of the pot—get every drop of it!
8. To make the crispy topping, combine the nutritional yeast, smoked paprika, pepper, and salt in a bowl. Pour the melted butter into the breadcrumb mix and stir until all the butter is absorbed.
9. Sprinkle the breadcrumb butter mixture evenly on top of the pasta.
10. Bake, uncovered, for 20 to 30 minutes, until the breadcrumb topping gets golden and crispy. Let cool for about 10 minutes before serving.

CREAMY TOFU AND BROCCOLI BAKE

SERVES 6 TO 8

Think chicken and broccoli casserole, elevated. This dish has meaty tofu, broccoli, and rice smothered in a creamy mushroom sauce and topped with vegan cheese. It's so delicious and satisfying, perfect for your sweater season gatherings, tailgates, and potlucks.

Tofu "chicken"

2 14-ounce blocks extra-firm tofu, drained and pressed
⅓ cup nutritional yeast
½ tablespoon garlic powder
½ tablespoon onion powder
1 teaspoon black pepper
½ teaspoon salt

Mushroom cream sauce

1 ½ cups raw unsalted cashews
1 cup vegan chicken broth or vegetable broth
2 tablespoons extra-virgin olive oil
1 small yellow onion, diced
2 stalks celery, diced
8 ounces cremini mushrooms, thinly sliced
3 cloves garlic, minced
¼ cup dry white wine or cooking wine
1 tablespoon soy sauce (can sub tamari or coconut aminos)
½ teaspoon black pepper
¼ teaspoon salt

1. Preheat the oven to 350°F and line a baking sheet with parchment paper; set aside.
2. To make the tofu chicken, cut the tofu into bite-size cubes.
3. Add the tofu chicken seasonings in a large bowl and stir to combine. Add the tofu to the bowl and, using a spoon or your hands, coat the tofu with the seasonings. *I like to use a large sealable container so I can shake the tofu around in the seasonings.*
4. Spread out the tofu on the baking sheet and bake for 35 minutes. While the tofu is baking, start the mushroom cream sauce. Remove the tofu when done and set aside. Keep the oven set to 350°F.
5. To make the cream sauce, add the cashews to a bowl and pour boiling water over them, enough to cover. Let them sit for at least 15 minutes.
6. Drain and add cashews to a high-speed blender or food processor. Add the broth to the blender and blend on high until you have a smooth cashew cream. There should be no more chunks of cashew left. Set the cream aside.
7. Heat oil in a pan over medium heat. Add onions and celery and sauté, stirring occasionally, until tender, about 5 to 7 minutes.

recipe and ingredients continue

recipe continued from previous page

Casserole

4 cups cooked white rice (can sub brown)
2 cups cooked broccoli florets, roughly chopped to bite size
1⅓ cup vegan shredded cheddar cheese, divided

8. Add the mushrooms and sauté until they release their moisture, about 5 minutes. Turn up the heat to medium-high and continue to sauté until the moisture evaporates, about another 4 minutes.
9. Add the garlic and sauté for another minute, stirring frequently.
10. Lastly, add the wine, soy sauce, pepper, and salt. Reduce temp to medium-low and let simmer for 2 minutes. Remove from heat.
11. Take the cashew cream and pour it into the pan with the mushrooms, stirring it until it is evenly combined.
12. To assemble the casserole, combine the rice, broccoli, 1 cup of the cheese, the mushroom sauce, and the tofu in a large mixing bowl. Gently stir until it is evenly combined.
13. Transfer to a 9x13-inch, or similar-sized, baking dish. Top with the remaining ⅓ cup of cheese.
14. Bake at 350°F for 20 to 25 minutes, until the cheese on top is melted. Let cool for about 15 minutes before serving.

Party tip

This dish can be assembled and refrigerated, prior to baking, the day before your party. Keep it covered while in the refrigerator and let it sit out for about 30 minutes before baking.

SPINACH GNOCCHI WITH PESTO ROSSO

SERVES 6 TO 8 (MAKES ABOUT 120 GNOCCHI)

Tender gnocchi smothered in a sweet, spicy, and tangy pesto rosso (red pesto). Though the gorgeous green and red make it fitting for the holiday season, this dish is great all year long!

2 pounds russet potatoes
3 ounces fresh spinach
1 ¼ cup all-purpose flour
½ teaspoon salt
½ teaspoon garlic powder
½ teaspoon onion powder

Pesto rosso sauce
1 cup sun-dried tomatoes in oil
1 cup fresh basil
⅓ cup walnuts
2 garlic cloves
½ teaspoon kosher salt
½ teaspoon crushed red pepper flakes (omit if you don't want heat)
½ to ¾ cup extra-virgin olive oil

1. Preheat oven to 400°F and line a baking sheet with tin foil. Pierce the potatoes with a fork about 8 to 10 times and place them on the baking sheets. Bake for 60 minutes, until potatoes are tender. Remove from oven.
2. Once the potatoes are cool enough to be handled, cut the potatoes in half and scoop the potato flesh out of each potato into a potato ricer or mixing bowl.
3. Run the potatoes through a potato ricer into a mixing bowl or mash the potatoes with a masher or a fork until they are completely mashed, with no, or very little, chunks remaining. You can also use an electric hand mixer; just make sure to stop mixing as soon as the potatoes are mashed; do not overmix or the dumplings will be less pillowy and instead dense.
4. Bring a small pot of water to boil. Add the spinach and boil until tender, about 3 minutes.
5. Drain spinach and transfer to a high-speed blender or food processor. Pulse until pureed. You may need to add a tablespoon of water if the spinach is getting stuck in the blender.
6. Pour the spinach into the potatoes and stir until evenly combined.
7. In a separate bowl, whisk together the flour, salt, garlic, and onion powder. Add the seasoned flour to the potatoes and stir together with a spoon until you reach cookie dough consistency. You may need to use your hands to finish mixing.

recipe continues

recipe continued from previous page

8. Cut or break off a piece of the dough and roll it into a thin log, about ½ inch thick. Cut 1-inch-long pieces and set aside. Continue this until you have used all the dough.
9. Optional step: Want marks on your gnocchi? Hold a fork in one hand with the end of the prongs touching the counter or a plate. With the other hand, place gnocchi at the base of the fork prongs. Use your thumb to gently push and roll the gnocchi down the fork to the plate or counter. It may take you a couple to get the hang of it.
10. Bring a pot of lightly salted water to boil. Add gnocchi in batches and boil for about 3 minutes; once they float, give them another 30 to 45 seconds. Remove gnocchi with a slotted spoon and add to a bowl with the pesto rosso sauce. Gently stir to combine.
11. Transfer to your serving dish and serve with a serving spoon or toothpicks. This dish is great warm, at room temperature, and chilled!

Pesto rosso sauce

1. Add the sun-dried tomatoes, basil, walnuts, garlic, salt, and crushed red pepper flakes (if using) to a food processor and process on low or pulse mode until you get a paste. You will have to scrape down the sides a few times.
2. Drizzle ½ cup of extra-virgin olive oil into the sauce as the processor continues to process on low. If you want it to be thinner, add the remaining oil.

Party tip

Make the gnocchi the day before you want to serve them, but do not boil them. Instead, arrange them on a sheet pan, dust them lightly with flour, and cover with a clean towel or plastic wrap. Store in the refrigerator. Pesto rosso can be made up to 5 days in advance and stored in an airtight container in the refrigerator. On the day of your party, allow the pesto to come to room temperature, boil the gnocchi, combine, and serve!

SAUCE ON THE SIDE

AGAVE MUSTARD

MAKES ABOUT 1 CUP

Even better than with honey! This sweet, tangy, creamy sauce goes on everything.

½ cup vegan mayonnaise
2 tablespoons agave nectar
2 teaspoons white wine vinegar
½ teaspoon salt
4 tablespoons Dijon mustard
2 tablespoons yellow mustard

1. Mix it all up in a bowl. Best when chilled in the refrigerator for at least an hour before serving. Store in an airtight container for up to 4 days.

Party tip
Make up to 4 days ahead of your party and store in an airtight container in the refrigerator.

BUFFALO SAUCE

MAKES 1 ½ CUPS

Classic spicy, tangy sauce for vegan nuggets, fries, tots, veggies, wraps, salads, and so much more!

1 cup hot pepper sauce (such as Frank's RedHot)
½ cup vegan butter
1 ½ tablespoons white vinegar
1 teaspoon vegan Worcestershire sauce
½ teaspoon garlic powder
¼ teaspoon salt, if butter was unsalted

1. Combine everything in a small saucepan and heat over medium heat.
2. Bring to a simmer, stirring frequently with a whisk.
3. When the sauce starts to bubble on the sides, remove from heat. Stir again with the whisk, and then the sauce is ready to use!

Party tip
Make this sauce up to 5 days in advance of your party and store it in an airtight container in the refrigerator. Reheat in a saucepan over medium-low heat, stirring frequently, or microwave in 30-second increments, stirring each time.

CHEESY SAUCE

MAKES ABOUT 3 ½ CUPS

Pour this sauce over your fries, tots, veggies, or nachos; use it as a dip for soft pretzels, or just slurp it up with a spoon, this is guilt-free cheese sauce!

- 2 cups russet potato (about 1 large), peeled and chopped
- 1 cup carrots (about 2 or 3), peeled and chopped
- 1 ½ cups unsweetened non-dairy milk
- ½ cup nutritional yeast
- 2 tablespoons olive oil
- 1 tablespoon cornstarch
- 1 tablespoon lemon juice
- ½ teaspoon garlic powder
- ½ teaspoon Old Bay seasoning
- ½ teaspoon smoked paprika
- ½ teaspoon onion powder
- ½ teaspoon salt

1. Place the potatoes and carrots in a medium pot and cover with water. Bring to a boil on high heat. Once boiling, reduce heat to a simmer and cook until potatoes and carrots are soft, about 15 to 20 minutes.
2. Drain the potatoes and carrots and add them to a high-speed blender along with the remaining ingredients.
3. Blend on high until smooth. Store leftover cheese sauce in an airtight container in the refrigerator for up to 5 days.

Party tip

Make this sauce up to 5 days before your party and store it in an airtight container. Reheat in a saucepan over medium-low heat, stirring frequently, or microwave in 30-second increments, stirring each time.

FRY SAUCE

MAKES 1 ½ CUPS

This is not just for fries or tots; this sauce is great for vegan tenders, vegan burgers, vegan hot dogs, sandwiches, and wraps. I've even used it for pierogi!

- 1 cup vegan mayonnaise
- ½ cup ketchup
- 1 tablespoon jalapeño brine
- ½ teaspoon smoked paprika
- ½ teaspoon kosher salt

1. Stir it all up together. Refrigerate for at least 30 minutes before serving. Serve cold as a dip or spread.

Party tip

Make this sauce up to 4 days in advance of your party and store it in an airtight container in the refrigerator.

RANCH

MAKES 2 CUPS

Great for chips, pretzels, veggies, vegan nuggets, sandwiches, wraps, pinwheels—is there anything ranch doesn't go well with?

1 cup vegan mayonnaise
1 cup vegan sour cream
1 tablespoon lemon juice
1 ¼ teaspoon dried dill
1 teaspoon dried chives
1 teaspoon dried parsley
1 teaspoon garlic powder
1 teaspoon onion powder
½ teaspoon salt
½ teaspoon black pepper

1. Combine everything together. Done!

Party tip
Letting the dip chill allows the flavors to blend together, so make this dip ahead and store it in an airtight container in the refrigerator for up to 5 days.

BANG BANG SAUCE

MAKES 1 ½ CUPS

It's not just for shrimp. This creamy, sweet, and spicy sauce goes great with tofu, veggies, vegan nuggets, fries and tots, vegan sushi, you name it. Get dipping!

1 cup vegan mayonnaise
½ cup Thai sweet chili sauce
2 tablespoons Sriracha sauce
2 teaspoon agave nectar

1. Stir it all up together. Done!

Party tip
Make up to 4 days in advance of your party and store in an airtight container in the refrigerator.

BBQ SAUCE

MAKES 3 CUPS

Sweet and tangy BBQ sauce. Use it as a dip, a marinade, a sauce for pizza, a burger spread, or a salad dressing, this sauce goes with everything.

1 cup tomato sauce
1 cup ketchup
⅓ cup light brown sugar
2 tablespoon agave nectar
⅔ cup apple cider vinegar
½ teaspoon salt
½ teaspoon onion powder
½ teaspoon garlic powder
½ teaspoon black pepper
¼ teaspoon chili powder

1. Add all the above ingredients to a medium saucepan over medium-high heat and stir until smooth.
2. Continue to cook, stirring frequently, until the sauce begins to boil, then reduce the heat to a simmer.
3. Simmer for 30 minutes, while continuing to stir occasionally.
4. Remove from heat. Sauce will continue to thicken as it cools.

Party tip

This sauce can be made 1 week in advance of your party. Store in an airtight container in the refrigerator. If you want to serve it warm, reheat it in a saucepan on medium-low heat, stirring occasionally, or in the microwave for 30-second intervals, stirring after each.

HOT AGAVE

MAKES 1 CUP

Meet Hot Agave, hot honey's cousin. Perfectly sweet and spicy and goes on just about anything. Drizzle away!

1 cup agave nectar
1 tablespoon crushed red pepper flakes
1 teaspoon garlic powder
1 pinch salt
2 teaspoons apple cider vinegar
2 teaspoons vinegar-based hot sauce (*I use Tabasco*)

1. Combine the agave nectar, chili flakes, garlic powder, and salt in a small saucepan over low heat.
2. Bring to a gentle simmer for 1 to 2 minutes, stirring frequently.
3. Remove from heat and allow to cool for about 3 to 5 minutes, then stir in the vinegar and hot sauce.
4. Let the sauce continue to sit for another 10 to 20 minutes to allow the flavors to infuse.
5. For a smoother sauce, strain out the chili flakes with a fine mesh strainer (optional). If you leave the chili flakes in the sauce, it will continue to get spicier with time. Use immediately, or pour it into a jar and store it, sealed, in the refrigerator.

Party tip

This sauce can be made 1 week in advance of your party. Store in an airtight container in the refrigerator. If the sauce crystallizes in the refrigerator, let it sit on the counter for about 30 minutes until it comes to room temperature, or place the jar in a bowl of warm water.

DESSERTS

MINI KEY LIME PIES WITH COCONUT WHIPPED CREAM

MAKES 12 MINI PIES

Key lime pie: sweet and tangy, refreshing and creamy. There is nothing like it. Traditionally, key lime pie is made with eggs and milk. Luckily, we can recreate the ultimate summertime taste with silken tofu. Skeptical? This recipe has been approved by my non-vegan, key-lime-pie-loving family.

Crust

1 ¼ cups vegan graham cracker crumbs (approximately 1 sleeve graham crackers)
¼ cup vegan butter, melted

Filling

2 tablespoons lime zest (about 3 regular limes or 6 to 7 key limes), plus additional for garnish (optional)
1 cup fresh lime juice (about 8 to 10 regular limes or 18 to 20 key limes)*
8 ounces firm silken tofu
¾ cup coconut cream
½ cup agave nectar
4 tablespoons cornstarch
¼ tsp salt

Whipped cream (optional)

15-ounce can coconut cream
1 ½ cups powdered sugar
2 teaspoons clear vanilla flavor (can sub vanilla extract)

Crust

1. Preheat oven to 375°F and line a standard muffin tin with 12 cupcake liners.
2. Add graham crackers to a food processor and grind until crackers have become fine crumbs, with no big pieces remaining.
3. Add the melted butter and pulse again until evenly combined.
4. Spoon about 1 ½ tablespoons of the mixture into each baking cup. Using your fingers or a spoon, press down on the crumbs to create a level, flat base.
5. Bake for 10 to 12 minutes or until golden brown. Remove and set aside to cool.

Filling

1. Add the lime juice, tofu, coconut cream, cornstarch, agave, and salt in a blender or food processor and blend until smooth.
2. Pour the mixture into a small or medium saucepan over medium-high heat and add in the lime zest. Bring to a light boil, stirring or whisking constantly. Once the mixture thickens, remove from heat.
3. Pour the lime mixture into each of the graham cracker base cups. Use a spoon or knife to gently make each cup level.
4. Chill the cups in the refrigerator until they set, approximately 4 to 5 hours.
5. Optional: When ready to serve, top with a dollop of coconut whipped cream and a sprinkle of the lime zest.

recipe continues

recipe continued from previous page

Whipped cream

1. Place the can of coconut cream in the refrigerator for a couple hours prior to making the whipped cream.
2. Scoop the top layer of coconut cream fat from the can into a bowl, leaving the liquid in the can. Save the rest of the liquid—you're going to need that too in just a minute.
3. Cream the coconut cream fat using a hand mixer for about 3 minutes, until it is whipped.
4. Add the powdered sugar, vanilla flavor, and 1 tablespoon of the coconut liquid from the can. Continue to mix using the hand mixer for about 3 minutes. The consistency should be light and soft. If it is too dense, add more of the coconut liquid ½ tablespoon at a time, continuing to mix each time, until you get the consistency you desire.

Note

* Traditionally you should use key limes for a key lime pie; however, key limes can be hard to find offseason. No worries—regular limes taste great in this recipe too

Party Tip

The key lime pies and the whipped cream can be made up to 3 days in advance of your party and stored in an airtight container in the refrigerator, separately.

CHOCOLATE-COVERED PRETZELS

SERVES 6 TO 10

Salty pretzels in sweet chocolate and covered in your favorite toppings. Match the sprinkle color to the celebration. Multicolored for a birthday, gold for New Year's, your favorite team color on game day—so many possibilities!

3 cups pretzels
1 cup vegan chocolate chips (dark, dairy-free milk or white)
½ teaspoon coconut oil

Toppings (optional)
Additional batch of melted chocolate for drizzling
Crushed candy canes
Crushed Oreos
Crushed peanuts
Vegan sprinkles

1. Set up your dipping station first. Line a large baking sheet with parchment paper. Set aside. Get out your pretzels and sprinkles. Crush any candy or nuts or cookies that you are using and have them ready in a bowl.
2. There are 2 ways to melt the chocolate. Double broiler and microwave methods. *I prefer the microwave method.*
Double boiler method: Add an inch of water in a saucepan. Bring to a simmer on medium heat. Add the chocolate and coconut oil into a heat-safe bowl that fits inside the saucepan but does NOT touch the simmering water. Place the bowl inside the saucepan and stir the chocolate frequently as it melts.
Microwave method: Add the chocolate and coconut oil to a small- to medium-sized microwave-safe bowl. Microwave for 20 seconds and stir chocolate. Continue this process for 20 seconds at a time, stirring after, until the chocolate is smooth and fully melted.
3. Dip a pretzel in the melted chocolate. Lift the pretzel out of the chocolate using a fork, allowing the excess chocolate to drip off before placing the pretzel on the parchment paper-covered baking sheet.
4. Decorate the pretzel as desired. Continue with the remaining pretzels. Repeat the heating process if necessary. If you are drizzling a different chocolate on top of an already chocolate-dipped pretzel, allow the first chocolate to set in the fridge for 20 minutes before adding the drizzle.
5. Allow pretzels to set in the refrigerator for 30 minutes.

Party tip
Pretzels can be made up to 2 weeks before your party and stored in the refrigerator in an airtight container.

CHOCOLATE FONDUE

SERVES 8 TO 10

My favorite holiday dessert! The dairy has been upgraded to coconut cream for a smooth and decadent chocolate treat. Get dipping!

14-ounce can coconut cream
2 teaspoons pure vanilla extract
1 pinch of salt
20-ounce bag dairy-free chocolate chips

1. Add coconut cream, vanilla extract, and salt to a medium saucepan and heat over medium heat, stirring occasionally.
2. When it starts to bubble around the edges, add the chocolate and lower the heat to medium-low.
3. Heat fondue, stirring frequently until chocolate is fully melted.
4. Transfer to a fondue pot and serve with your favorite dippers like apples, bananas, strawberries, pretzels, or vegan cookies.

Note

Don't have a fondue pot? No worries! You can keep the fondue in the saucepan and place it on a trivet. You will have to keep reheating on the stove as the chocolate hardens. Another option is to use a small slow cooker on warm heat. Or use a regular-sized slow cooker and just double or triple this recipe—is there such a thing as too much chocolate? The answer is NO.

Party tip

You can make this fondue up to 3 days before your party and store it in an airtight container in the refrigerator. Simply reheat in a saucepan on low heat, stirring frequently.

LEMON BLUEBERRY COOKIES

MAKES ABOUT 24 COOKIES

These soft, chewy, melt-in-your-mouth cookies have a vibrant lemon flavor with bursts of sweet blueberries.

1 tablespoon ground flaxseed meal
3 tablespoons water
1 cup salted vegan butter, softened but still cold (in stick or block form)
1 cup granulated sugar
¼ cup light brown sugar
Lemon zest from 2 lemons (about 1 heaping tablespoon)
1 teaspoon lemon extract
2 ½ cups all-purpose flour
½ teaspoon baking soda
½ teaspoon salt
½ cup frozen wild blueberries (keep in freezer until ready to mix into dough)

1. Preheat the oven to 350°F and line 1 or 2 baking sheets with parchment paper. Set aside.
2. Add the ground flaxseed meal and water to a small bowl or cup and set aside. This will become your flax egg.
3. Cream together the butter and sugar using a stand mixer or electric hand mixer.
4. Add in the flax egg, zest, and lemon extract and mix again, scraping down the sides of the bowl to evenly combine.
5. Add the flour, baking soda, and salt, and mix until the dough forms. Chill the dough in the refrigerator for 30 minutes.
6. Fold in the frozen blueberries until evenly distributed. Purple streaks will appear as you mix the berries in. If the dough is mixed too much, the dough will turn completely purple *(it will still taste amazing, so don't worry if it happens)*
7. Scoop about 1 ½ tablespoons of dough onto the baking sheet(s), leaving about 2 inches of space between dough balls.
8. Bake for 11 to 15 minutes, until edges turn lightly golden.
9. Let the cookies cool on the pan for 5 minutes, then transfer to a wire cooling rack to finish cooling.

Party tip

Make these cookies up to 4 days before your party and store them in an airtight container at room temperature.

ICED OATMEAL COOKIES

MAKES ABOUT 18 COOKIES

Classic oatmeal cookies: chewy, satisfying, and always a hit. This batch has a hint of cinnamon and pumpkin pie spice and is topped with vanilla icing.

1 tablespoon ground flaxseed meal
3 tablespoons water
1 ¼ cup all-purpose flour
1 ¼ cup old-fashioned rolled oats
½ teaspoon baking powder
⅛ teaspoon baking soda
½ teaspoon salt
¼ teaspoon cinnamon
¼ teaspoon pumpkin pie spice
½ cup (1 stick) vegan butter, softened but still cool
1 cup (packed) dark brown sugar
1 teaspoon vanilla extract

Icing

¾ cup powdered sugar
1 ½ tablespoons non-dairy milk
½ teaspoon clear vanilla flavor (can sub vanilla extract)

Party tip

Make these cookies up to 3 days in advance of your party and store them in an airtight container at room temperature.

1. Mix flaxseed meal and water in a small bowl or cup and set aside. This will be your flax egg.
2. In a medium mixing bowl, whisk together the flour, oats, baking powder, baking soda, salt, cinnamon, and pumpkin spice. Set aside.
3. In a separate bowl, beat together the butter and brown sugar using an electric hand mixer or a stand mixer until creamy, about 2 to 3 minutes. Scrape down the sides of the bowl and add the flax egg and vanilla extract. Mix again for about 30 seconds, until evenly combined.
4. Now take the oats and flour bowl and add that to the butter and sugar bowl. Mix by hand or mixer on low speed just until combined. Place dough in refrigerator for 30 to 60 minutes.
5. Preheat oven to 350°F and line two baking sheets with parchment paper.
6. Once dough has chilled, scoop dough onto baking sheets, about 2 tablespoons per cookie, and place about 2 inches apart.
7. Bake for 11 to 13 minutes, until edges are slightly golden. Remove from the oven and let the cookies cool on the baking sheets for 5 minutes, then transfer the cookies to cooking racks to finish cooling.

Icing

1. Whisk the powdered sugar, milk, and vanilla together in a bowl until combined.
2. Once the cookies have completely cooled down, dip the top of the cookies into the icing and place them back on the cooling rack to set. If the icing is too thick to dip the cookies, add more non-dairy milk, 1 teaspoon at a time, until the desired consistency is reached.

CHOCOLATE MACADAMIA NUT COOKIES WITH SALTED CARAMEL

MAKES 12 LARGE COOKIES

Brown sugar, chocolate, macadamia nuts, and salted caramel. These cookies have it all. So decadent, your guests will be begging you to make them every year!

1 tablespoon ground flaxseed meal
3 tablespoons water
1 cup salted vegan butter, softened but still cold (in stick or block form)
1 cup brown sugar
½ cup granulated sugar
1 teaspoon vanilla
2 ¼ cups all-purpose flour
1 teaspoon baking soda
½ teaspoon salt
1 ½ cups chopped macadamia nuts
1 ½ cups dairy-free chocolate chips

Caramel sauce

½ cup cane sugar
⅔ cup canned full-fat coconut milk
½ teaspoon coarse sea salt

Party tip

These cookies can be made up to 3 days before your party and stored in an airtight container at room temperature.

1. Add flaxseed meal and water to a small bowl or cup and set aside. This will be your flax egg.
2. Cream together the butter and sugars until light and smooth using a stand mixer or electric mixer. This will take 2 to 3 minutes.
3. Scrape the sides of the bowl and mix in the flax egg and the vanilla.
4. In a separate mixing bowl, stir together the flour, baking soda, and salt. Gradually add the dry ingredients to the butter and sugar mixture, stirring until almost completely incorporated.
5. Fold in the macadamia nuts and chocolate chips and mix until all of the flour is incorporated and the chips and nuts are evenly distributed.
6. Chill dough in the refrigerator for 30 minutes. Preheat oven to 350°F and line a baking sheet with parchment paper.
7. Scoop a heaping ⅓ cup portion of dough onto the baking sheet. Repeat with the rest of the cookie dough. Bake for 13 to 15 minutes, until the edges start to turn golden brown. Remove from oven and let the cookies cool on the baking sheet for about 15 minutes.
8. Transfer to a cooling rack to cool completely.
9. Top cookies with a drizzle of caramel sauce.

Caramel sauce

1. Heat a pot over medium-high heat.
2. Add the sugar and stir continuously for 1 minute.
3. Stir in coconut milk and sea salt and bring to a boil.
4. Reduce heat to medium-low and maintain a simmer until caramel thickens, about 10 to 15 minutes, stirring occasionally.
5. Stir in sea salt and remove from heat. Set aside to cool.

STRAWBERRY CHEESECAKES

MAKES 12 MINI CAKES

These decadent dessert cakes have a rich and creamy strawberry cheese filling on top of a buttery graham cracker crust and a nostalgic, sweet strawberry and cookie crumb topping.

Crust

1 ¼ cups vegan graham cracker crumbs (approximately 1 sleeve graham crackers)
¼ cup vegan butter, melted

Filling

1 ⅓ cup canned coconut cream fat (the thick layer on top that separates when chilled)
¾ cup powdered sugar
2 tablespoons lemon juice
2 teaspoons vanilla extract
2 cups plain vegan cream cheese, softened
¾ cup freeze-dried strawberries, ground into powder in a food processor (you will need ¼ cup powder after processing)

Strawberry crunch topping

10 vegan vanilla sandwich cookies
1 cup freeze-dried strawberries
2 ½ tablespoon salted vegan butter, melted

Party tip

This dessert is make-ahead approved! The cakes need time to set, so make them up to 5 days in advance of your party and store them in the refrigerator covered.

Crust

1. Preheat oven to 375°F and line a standard muffin tin with 12 cupcake liners.
2. Add graham crackers to a food processor and grind until crackers have become fine crumbs, with no big pieces remaining.
3. Add the melted butter and pulse again until evenly combined.
4. Spoon about 1 ½ tablespoons of the mixture into each baking cup. Using your fingers or a spoon, press down on the crumbs to create a level, flat base.
5. Bake for 10 to 12 minutes or until golden brown. Remove and set aside to cool.

Filling

1. Whip the coconut cream in a bowl with a hand mixer until light.
2. Add the powdered sugar, lemon juice, and vanilla extract and continue to whip until well combined, light, and smooth.
3. Add cream cheese and strawberry powder and mix again until evenly combined.
4. Top the graham cracker crusts with the mixture. Use a spoon or a knife to gently make each cup level.
5. Chill the cups in the refrigerator until they set, at least 8 hours, preferably overnight.

Strawberry crunch topping

1. Add the cookies and the freeze-dried strawberries to a food processor and pulse until finely chopped.
2. Drizzle butter into the processor and pulse a few more times to combine.
3. Once the cheesecakes have set, top each of the cakes with the strawberry crunch topping.

RED VELVET CUPCAKES WITH CREAM CHEESE FROSTING

MAKES 12 CUPCAKES

Deliciously moist cupcakes with hints of cocoa and vanilla and that unmistakable red hue, topped with a rich and creamy frosting.

Dry ingredients

2 cups all-purpose plain flour
1 cup granulated sugar
2 tablespoons cocoa powder
2 ½ teaspoons baking powder
¼ teaspoon salt

Wet ingredients

1 cup non-dairy milk
⅓ cup vegetable oil (or another neutral-flavored oil)
¼ cup applesauce
2 tablespoons apple cider vinegar
2 teaspoons vanilla extract
1 teaspoon vegan red food coloring gel

Cream cheese frosting

1 cup vegan butter, room temperature
1 cup vegan cream cheese, room temperature
2 teaspoons vanilla extract
5 cups powdered sugar

Party tip

Make these cupcakes up to 3 days before your party and store them in an airtight container in the refrigerator.

Cupcake

1. Preheat the oven to 350°F and line a 12-cup standard muffin pan with cupcake liners.
2. In a large mixing bowl, add all the dry ingredients and mix until fully combined and there are no lumps.
3. In a separate bowl, combine all the wet ingredients, stirring until fully mixed.
4. Combine the dry and wet ingredients, and mix until you get a batter.
5. Spoon the batter equally into each cupcake liner; they should be ⅔ full.
6. Bake for 20 to 25 minutes. Check to see if they are done with the toothpick trick: insert a toothpick into the center of the cupcake. If it comes out clean with no wet batter, they are done.
7. Remove from heat, but keep cupcakes in the tin for about 5 minutes. Then transfer to a cooling rack to finish cooling. Wait until cupcakes have fully cooled before topping with frosting.

Frosting

1. Add the cream cheese, butter, and vanilla to a mixing bowl and beat until combined using an electric hand mixer (or stand mixer).
2. Add the sugar to the bowl and continue to mix until just combined; do not overmix. If frosting is not firm enough, add more sugar in ¼ cup increments.
3. Cover and keep in the refrigerator until ready to use. Top cupcakes with frosting using a spatula or a piping bag.

VANILLA SHEET CAKE WITH BUTTERCREAM FROSTING

SERVES 15 TO 20

Break out the party hats and blow up the balloons—it's party time!

Cake

2 cups coconut milk, room temperature (can sub another nondairy milk)
2 tablespoons apple cider vinegar
3 cups all-purpose flour
1 cup brown sugar
1 cup cane sugar
2 teaspoons baking soda
1 teaspoon salt
⅔ cup vegan butter, melted and cooled
1 ½ tablespoons vanilla extract

Buttercream frosting

1 cup vegan butter, softened
1 tablespoon vanilla extract
3 cups powdered sugar
1 tablespoon non-dairy milk, more if needed
¼ teaspoon salt, if using unsalted butter

Cake

1. Preheat the oven to 350°F and line a 9x13 sheet pan with parchment paper or grease with cooking spray.
2. In a small bowl, combine the coconut milk and apple cider vinegar, stir, and set aside. It will begin to curdle.
3. Whisk together flour, sugar, baking soda, and salt in a large bowl until thoroughly combined.
4. Add milk mixture, melted butter, and vanilla. Beat with an electric mixer on medium speed until just combined, about 1 to 2 minutes; do not overmix.
5. Pour the cake batter into the pan. Give the pan a tap on the counter a few times to remove any air bubbles.
6. Place the pan in the center of the middle rack of your oven. Bake for 30 to 35 minutes until fully baked; check by inserting a toothpick into the center of the cake; if it comes out clean, it is done. Remove the cake from the oven and let it cool completely in the pan.
7. After the cake has cooled, remove it from the pan, cover with buttercream frosting, and decorate with candles, fresh fruit, or vegan sprinkles. Enjoy!

recipe continues

recipe continued from previous page

Frosting

1. In a mixing bowl, add the butter and the vanilla extract and mix with an electric mixer until they are fully combined and fluffy, about 2 minutes at medium speed.
2. Add 1 cup of the powdered sugar and mix at low speed until combined. Repeat, adding 1 cup of sugar at a time until all the sugar is incorporated. If you used unsalted butter, mix in the salt as well.
3. Add the milk. Set the mixer back to medium and mix the frosting until it is light and fluffy. If the frosting is too thin, add more sugar, 1 to 2 tablespoons at a time. Add extra milk, ½ tablespoon at a time, if it's too thick.
4. Once you get your desired consistency, ice the cake and decorate!

Party tip

Make this birthday cake up to 3 days in advance of your party and store it, covered, at room temperature. If you are decorating it with fresh fruit, wait until serving to add it and store it in the refrigerator.

BROWNIES

SERVES 8 TO 12

Rich, chocolatey goodness. It's the ultimate comfort dessert food and perfect for any occasion.

1 ½ cups all-purpose flour
8 tablespoons dark Dutch-processed cocoa powder
1 ½ cups cane sugar
½ cup aquafaba (liquid from a can of chickpeas)*
1 tablespoon pure vanilla extract
½ tsp sea salt
9 ounces dark chocolate chips or vegan milk chocolate chips, divided**
8 tablespoons vegan butter

Note
**I like to use different brands of dark or vegan milk chocolate chips to add some depth to the flavor. For example, I used 6 ounces dark chocolate chips to melt into the batter, and I added 3 ounces vegan milk chocolate chips to fold in at the end. Optional, but it adds a little extra yum!

Party tip
Make brownies up to 3 days in advance of your party and store them in an airtight container at room temperature.
*Don't waste the chickpeas! Check out hummus recipes on pages 67 and 68.

1. Preheat the oven to 350°F and line an 8x8-inch baking pan, or similar size, with parchment paper. Make sure the parchment paper hangs slightly over the sides so you can later lift the brownies easily.
2. In a medium mixing bowl, add the flour and the cocoa powder together. Use a whisk to ensure that it is evenly combined and there are no lumps.
3. In a large mixing bowl, add the sugar and aquafaba. Use a stand mixer or electric mixer to mix the two together until they are combined, thickened, and wavy, approximately 3 minutes.
4. Add the vanilla and salt to the aquafaba mixture and stir to combine.
5. Add 6 ounces of dark chocolate chips and the butter to a microwave-friendly bowl. Microwave on high for 30 seconds. Stir the chocolate, then microwave for 30 seconds and stir again until the chocolate and butter are evenly melted together. This will take approximately 1 ½ to 2 minutes. Pour the melted chocolate into the aquafaba mixture and stir until evenly distributed.
6. Add the flour and cocoa powder mix to the wet ingredients. Stir until combined and you do not see dry flour.
7. Lastly, add the remaining chocolate chips and fold them into the batter.
8. Transfer the batter into the pan. Use a spatula or the back of a spoon to smooth the top of the batter so it is evenly distributed in the pan.
9. Bake uncovered for 35 to 40 minutes; check if it is done by inserting a toothpick in the center of the brownies; the toothpick should come out without batter. Melted chocolate is expected, but if the batter is still wet, let the brownies cook more and check in another 5 minutes.
10. Remove from heat and let the brownies cool in the pan for about 25 minutes.
11. Using the parchment paper edges, carefully pull the brownies out of the pan and allow them to cool on a wire rack for another 20 minutes. Cut into desired piece sizes and enjoy!

21-AND-OVER ORANGE CREAMSICLE

SERVES 2

Classic flavor combo, just like the childhood ice cream bar, but this one is just for the adults.

3 ounces whipped cream vodka (can sub vanilla vodka)
3 ounces fresh orange juice*
3 ounces coconut milk
1 ounce triple sec

Garnish (optional)
Orange slice

1. Fill a shaker with ice.
2. Add vodka, orange juice, coconut milk, and triple sec. Shake well.
3. Pour into glasses over new ice and garnish with an orange slice. CHEERS!

Note
*Fresh squeezed orange juice is best, but store-bought works great too. If using fresh, 1 medium orange produces approximately 2 to 3 ounces of juice.

BOOZY HOT CHOCOLATE

SERVES 2

Creamy, rich, and so chocolaty. This adult treat is perfect for your holiday party!

13.5-ounce can coconut milk
6 ounces vegan dark chocolate chips
3 ounces vanilla vodka
½ teaspoon vanilla extract
1 pinch kosher salt

Garnish (optional)
Crushed peppermint rim
Candy canes
Dark chocolate shavings
Mini vegan marshmallows
Vegan sprinkles
Whipped coconut cream

1. Add the coconut milk to a small saucepan and heat over medium-low heat.
2. When milk starts to simmer, add the chocolate chips and whisk continuously until the chocolate is melted and smooth, about 5 minutes.
3. Remove from heat and stir in the vodka, vanilla extract, and salt.
4. Allow the hot chocolate to sit for a few minutes and cool to a safe drinking temperature.
5. Pour into 2 heatproof glasses or mugs and top with some vegan whipped cream and shave a dark chocolate bar on top! Or add mini candy canes or vegan mini marshmallows and some sprinkles—get festive! CHEERS!

Thank you

This has been a dream of mine for years…

To my husband, Patrick: Thank you for your unwavering love and patience as I reinvented myself to find this path. Every time I stumbled, you told me to keep going. Whenever I was nervous, you simply said, "Good, that means you care. It's a good thing to be nervous." I carry those words with me in everything I do. I love you with all my heart!

To my mother, Robbin: Thank you for hosting our family holidays; you gave me my passion for cooking. Thank you for being my biggest cheerleader. I wish everyone could have someone who believes in them the way you believe in me!

To my brother, Jerid: This project started after that profound and clarifying conversation we had about living our lives today the way we want them to be in the future. That talk changed everything. Your check-ins proved you believed I could achieve this goal even when I doubted myself. Thank you, bro!

To Ava, Owen, Declan, and Emilia: Thank you for giving me the drive to be an aunt and GG you can be proud of and to be an example for you to keep working for your dreams, no matter how long it takes.

Kara, thank you for your constant support, love, and friendship.

Thank you to my fur babies, Guinness and Kelce Foles, for giving me endless love and for being the reason I went vegan in the first place.

Thank you to Robin Arzón, my favorite Peloton instructor, whom I have never met but whose words play on repeat in my head: "You're not too old; it's not too late."

And the biggest thank you of all is to you. Thank you for helping to make my dream come true. I hope that this book finds you well and that you continue to work toward making your dreams come true. Maybe you can use some of these recipes when you are celebrating your next big win!

Have fun!

♡ Elisa

Index

Index

www.ingramcontent.com/pod-product-compliance
Ingram Content Group UK Ltd.
Pitfield, Milton Keynes, MK11 3LW, UK
UKHW060121010826
14089UKWH00006B/94

9 798993 720906